inside AIDS

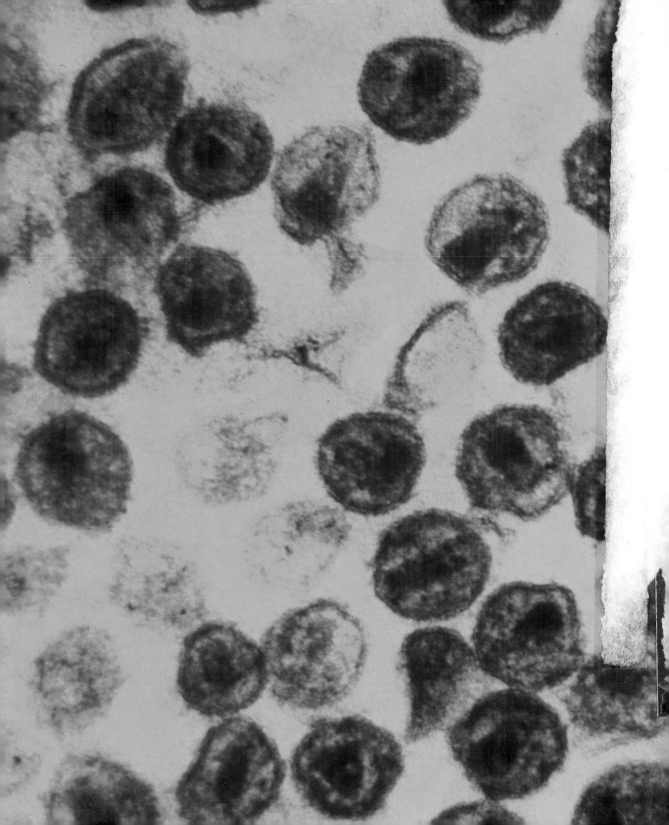

inside
AIDS
HIV Attacks the Immune System

Conrad J. Storad

Lerner Publications Company • Minneapolis

For the millions of young people living with the specter of HIV infection and AIDS. In hope, there is strength.

This book is the product of more than five years of effort. Many people helped me to get this work into print. While I cannot acknowledge all by name in this space, I am indebted to the scholarly efforts of many scientists and physicians, and to the superb interpretive work of science journalists whose writing served as important background for this book. Special thanks go to my editors, Ruth Berman and Susan Breckner Rose, who kept the project alive when I was ready to call it quits. Thanks also go to the many professional public information officers at the National Institutes of Health, Centers for Disease Control, World Health Organization, and the Joint United Nations Program on HIV/AIDS who provided volumes of background material and up-to-the-minute research findings. Special thanks go to Gregory K. Folkers, Patricia Randall, and Joe Bangiolo at the National Institute for Allergy and Infectious Diseases; Patricia Newman at the National Cancer Institute; and Allahina Russell at the World Health Organization.

Lerner Publications Company
A Division of Lerner Publishing Group
241 First Avenue North
Minneapolis, MN 55401 U.S.A.

Website address: www.lernerbooks.com

Library of Congress Cataloging-in-Publication Data

Storad, Conrad J.
   Inside AIDS : HIV attacks the immune system / Conrad J. Storad
     p.   cm.
   Includes bibliographical references and index.
   Summary: Discusses the reaction of the human body to viruses, the
 AIDS virus (HIV), and its effect on the human immune system.
   ISBN 0-8225-2857-6 (alk. paper)
   1. AIDS (Disease)—Juvenile literature. [1. AIDS (Disease)
 2. Diseases.] I. Title.
 RC607.A26S755 1998
 616.97'92—dc21   97–41570

Manufactured in the United States of America
2 3 4 5 6 7 – JR – 05 04 03 02 01 00

Contents

Preface

Growing up is difficult. The threat of AIDS and other sexually transmitted diseases has made growing up a lot harder. A big part of growing up is learning how to take responsibility for yourself, for your decisions, and for your actions. Every day brings new challenges and new decisions to make. As a teenager, you learn how to get along with your parents and family. You learn how to deal with teachers, friends, and all kinds of other people. You learn how to manage your money. And to stay healthy, you need to learn how to take responsibility for your own body, especially when it comes to learning about sexual matters.

New information about AIDS and HIV, the virus that causes AIDS, continues to arrive every day. Scientists are expending a huge amount of human brain power in an effort to understand the disease. When I first began this project in 1993, there was not much good news to report concerning AIDS. In late 1996, for the first time since the epidemic began, medical researchers finally had something to cheer about in the battle against this killer disease. While there still is no cure in sight, certain combinations of powerful drugs and other treatment techniques have offered a glimmer of hope. Early results from several studies indicate that these treatments appear to be effective at slowing HIV's ability to reproduce inside the human body.

Research continues at a frantic pace. This book is an attempt to provide you with a bit of useful information about how AIDS works as a disease. I've tried to provide a condensed version of a portion of the most current information available by consulting hundreds of sources. Scientists continue to learn more about HIV and AIDS even as you read these words. As a result, new developments and discoveries will continue to occur after this book has gone to press. New discoveries often result in changes to the information scientists and physicians already thought they knew. To date, however, one scary fact remains rock solid. If you become infected with HIV and develop AIDS, you will die of AIDS complications.

In 1996, AIDS became the number-one killer of young Americans. AIDS now kills one of every five Americans who die between the ages of 25 and 44. But the picture is a bit more complicated because infection with HIV does not kill overnight. The virus can slowly reproduce inside apparently healthy people for as long as 10 years before erupting into AIDS. This means that most 25-year-olds who die of AIDS caught the virus when they were teenagers. The most likely source of that infection was engaging in sex without the protection of a condom or injecting drugs with a dirty needle.

Other numbers are even scarier. The Centers for Disease Control in Atlanta estimates that more than 25 percent of all new HIV infections in the United States occur in young people between the ages of 13 and 20. That means that two Americans under the age of 20 become infected with HIV every hour of every day. Worldwide, 11 people are infected with HIV each and every minute, according to the Joint United Nations Program on HIV/AIDS.

Perhaps people have come to expect too much from science

and medicine. We expect the truth, and we expect full answers, quickly. After all, isn't that the way it works on television or in the movies? TV doctors and motion-picture scientists usually manage to find the cure or the answer to any medical mystery before a program ends. Unfortunately, that is not how things work in the real world. Research takes time and money and lots of hard work. Each new bit of information learned can result in a dozen new questions in need of answers.

So just how can you protect yourself from HIV and AIDS? Actually, it is a fairly simple process. First, you must learn to gather information and then transform it into useful knowledge. Then comes the hard part. You must learn how best to use that new knowledge in everyday life and take responsibility for your own actions.

The information is available. The choice is up to you.

Conrad J. Storad
Tempe, Arizona—December 1997

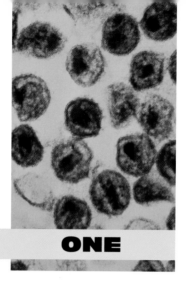

ONE

Roots of the Epidemic

We are living in the middle of an epidemic. A killer disease is here. The disease is called acquired immunodeficiency syndrome—AIDS for short. Once thought to be a disease that infected only homosexual men, we now know that AIDS can infect, and kill, most anyone.

Sarah is 10 years old. She lives in Phoenix, Arizona. She has a dog and two cats. She likes to draw. Sarah has AIDS.

Eric is 14. He likes to read and play computer games. He lives in Fresno, California. Eric has AIDS.

Debbie is 20. She lives in Lexington, Kentucky. A year ago, Debbie's infant daughter Shannon died from AIDS a month before her first birthday. Debbie also has AIDS.

Ramón is 13. He came to the United States from Mexico with his mother and two sisters in 1992. They live in Houston, Texas. He likes to play basketball and is pretty good on rollerblades. Ramón has AIDS.

Danika is 15 years old. Her mother is from the Philippines.

Her father is a sergeant in the U.S. Air Force. They live in Dayton, Ohio. Danika is a cheerleader at her junior high school. She wants to be a civil engineer. Danika has AIDS.

Sarah, Eric, Debbie, Shannon, Ramón, and Danika are real people. Their names have been changed. But their stories, and hundreds of others like theirs, have appeared in newspapers, magazines, on radio and television, and in books during the past decade. Each is representative of the thousands of young people living with AIDS in the United States.

AIDS was first reported in the United States in 1981. Since that time, the disease has become a worldwide epidemic. A disease is classified as an epidemic when it affects a large number of people within a certain population or region at the same time. AIDS is now considered to be a pandemic—it affects people living in countries in all parts of the world.

More than 6 billion people live on earth. In December 1997, the World Health Organization (WHO) reported that an estimated 30.6 million people worldwide had been infected with human immunodeficiency virus (HIV), the virus that causes AIDS. Almost 11.7 million people that we know of, including 2.7 million children, have died from complications due to AIDS.

The true number of people with this disease is difficult to calculate. Many countries have poor public health-care programs with unreliable reporting systems. Some have none at all. So to be conservative, WHO estimates that the number of people infected with HIV will increase from 30.6 million to between 40 and 110 million before the year 2000. They also report that the disease is spreading among populations of people living in every corner of our planet. AIDS will not be going away anytime soon.

In the United States, statistics provided by the federal government's Centers for Disease Control (CDC) indicate that an American is infected with HIV every 13 minutes. Someone dies of AIDS every 17 minutes. Since 1981, more than 500,000 Americans have been reported with AIDS. At least 300,000 have died from AIDS in the United States. That is more than five times the number of Americans who were killed during the Vietnam War.

Scientists have learned much about AIDS since 1981. They know that AIDS is caused by a virus invisible to the human eye. The virus that causes AIDS—HIV—is so small that it takes a powerful electron microscope just to see its outline. It is so small that thousands could fit on the period at the end of this sentence.

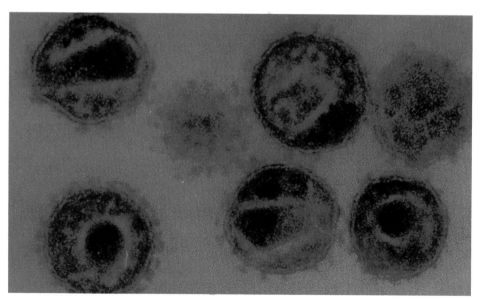

These particles of HIV have been magnified over a million times.

AIDS first caught the attention of scientists and physicians in 1981. At that time, doctors in California noticed an unusual number of people with a dangerous but rare infection called Pneumocystis carinii pneumonia (PCP).

Usually, a healthy immune system—which rids the body of any foreign, and potentially harmful, invaders—keeps PCP from infecting the body. But PCP can infect people who have organ transplants. Physicians give transplant patients powerful drugs to suppress, or block, their immune systems. This is so that the person's own body does not identify the newly transplanted organ as a foreign invader and try to reject it. As a result, the bodies of transplant patients are more vulnerable than healthy people to diseases like PCP.

Physicians often use drugs known as antibiotics to kill the bacteria and other germs that cause infections. Antibiotics are used to cure PCP when it develops in people who have had transplant operations. In 1981, antibiotics did not cure the PCP in the people being treated at the California hospitals.

Scientists at the CDC are the disease watchdogs for the United States. Hospitals and medical centers in every state routinely send reports of unusual diseases to CDC headquarters in Atlanta, Georgia. The CDC scientists pay close attention to reports of unusual infections and rare diseases. When the reports about people with PCP not responding to antibiotics continued to come in from California, the CDC decided to investigate. The scientists found that the patients had one other thing in common: they were all homosexual men.

As the investigation continued, the CDC found more and more cases of mysterious infections usually found only in people with weakened immune systems. Again, all the patients were homosexual men. The scientists guessed that these men were victims of some new kind of acquired disease, a disease passed from one person to another. Because all the patients had illnesses normally linked to weakened immune systems, the scientists named the mysterious new disease acquired immunodeficiency syndrome. It quickly became known by its acronym—AIDS.

Since the first cases of AIDS were seen only in homosexual men, many people began calling the disease the "gay plague," the "gay cancer," or GRID, short for gay-related immunodeficiency disease. At first, the disease received little attention from the media. That all changed when the disease began to show up in the sexual partners of AIDS patients and people who used intravenous drugs. Intravenous (IV) drugs are injected into the body with needles. The people who use IV drugs often share needles with other drug users. More and more IV drug users began to show the symptoms of AIDS.

The clues were increasing. The people coming down with AIDS were having sexual contact with lots of people or they were sharing IV drug needles.

Soon AIDS began to appear in a third group, people with hemophilia. A rare, inherited disease, hemophilia prevents blood from clotting when a person is cut or bruised. Hemophiliacs can easily bleed to death if they are cut or injured and not treated quickly.

The hemophiliacs who contracted AIDS posed a confusing question. What was the connection? The key was that hemophiliacs need regular transfusions of blood to get a blood product called Factor VIII, which helps blood to clot. Perhaps AIDS was transmitted in blood. Physicians started looking for an infectious agent. Perhaps some type of bacteria or virus might be the cause of AIDS. They needed proof.

Two separate teams of scientists—one French, one American—were the first to discover that a virus causes AIDS. In 1983, Dr. Luc Montagnier and other French researchers working at the Pasteur Institute in Paris found a virus in blood samples taken from an AIDS patient. They believed the virus was the cause of AIDS.

But few other scientists believed them. Many still thought that some factor in the gay lifestyle caused AIDS. The French group lacked the money to keep studying the virus they had found, so they froze their samples and stored them for later study.

A year later, in 1984, Dr. Robert Gallo and his team of scientists at the U.S. National Cancer Institute (NCI) in Bethesda, Maryland, found a virus that they believed to be the cause of AIDS. Both teams turned out to be correct. But the two groups got involved in a long legal fight over the right to claim discovery of the AIDS virus. Finally, in 1987, the French and American scientists agreed to list themselves as codiscover-

Dr. Robert Gallo and his assistants research the AIDS virus.

ers of the virus. They also agreed to name the virus HIV, short for human immunodeficiency virus.

Epidemiologists are scientists who study the spread of disease in groups of people. Looking back, these researchers know that AIDS was already present in the United States before 1981. Where it came from and why it started to kill people in large numbers are still questions without sure answers.

Most scientists agree that HIV is a new form of an old virus that infects apes and monkeys in parts of western and central Africa. The most widely accepted theory is that humans were first infected through direct contact with monkeys. Humans have hunted and handled monkeys for thousands of years in Africa. Anyone who was bitten or scratched, or who had gotten cut while butchering a monkey for a meal, could have been the first human infected with the virus. When might the first transmission from monkey to human have taken place? No one is sure. Since AIDS is a new epidemic, scientists think that the virus responsible for the disease must first have been transmitted to humans within the past 30 years.

According to another theory, a tamer version of HIV has infected people in Africa for centuries. Recent mutations, or genetic changes, made the virus into a killer. Then during the 1960s and 1970s, regional wars and drought in Africa forced many people to move from their traditional village homes into squalid, crowded refugee camps. They carried the virus with them. The crowded conditions made it easier for the virus to spread from person to person. The growth of cities in West Africa also shifted huge populations into new living conditions. Infected people traveling to and from West African cities spread the virus to Europe, North America, and throughout the world.

In another theory, researchers think that Haitians who worked in Zaire and other central African countries during the 1970s probably were infected and brought the virus with them when they returned home to their native Caribbean island. Haiti was a favorite vacation spot for many homosexual men living in the United States. Some American vacationers may have contracted the disease in Haiti and then unknowingly spread it when they returned home.

Since 1984, scientists have learned that HIV destroys the human body's ability to fight off infections, certain cancers, and other illnesses by killing or weakening the cells of the immune system. People with AIDS are easy targets for deadly infections caused by germs that usually don't harm healthy people.

Based on over a decade of research, scientists have developed statistical models to forecast the spread of the disease. The CDC's most current statistical model suggests that at least 40,000 Americans are being infected with HIV each year. Because roughly the same number of people are dying each year from AIDS, the number of people living with HIV infection has remained relatively stable in the United States since 1990.

The newest numbers seem to indicate that more people are paying attention and learning how to protect themselves from becoming infected with HIV. Still, in 1996, the CDC reported 80,691 more cases of AIDS in the United States than were reported in 1995. A diagnosis of AIDS usually comes only about two years before death. In 1996, a total of 13,615 teenagers and young adults got this diagnosis.

AIDS is a disease that can infect anyone. Those already dead from AIDS include men, women, and children; homosexuals and heterosexuals; and people of every race, color, economic background, and religion. The most recent numbers issued by the CDC indicate certain trends for AIDS in the United States. The number of AIDS cases continues to increase overall, but the rate of increase varies among different groups of people. The number of AIDS cases is increasing most rapidly among people infected through heterosexual contact. Between 1993 and 1994, the number of AIDS cases increased

- *6 percent in men who had had sex with men*
- *5 percent in people who injected drugs*
- *17 percent in people who had had heterosexual sex*

Among racial and ethnic groups, African Americans and Hispanics are most affected by the epidemic. In 1995, the rate of reported AIDS cases was

- *92.6 per 100,000 African Americans*
- *46.2 per 100,000 Hispanics*
- *15.4 per 100,000 whites*
- *12.3 per 100,000 Native Americans*

The CDC's numbers also indicate trends for AIDS among young and middle-aged adults, and among teenagers. As many as half of all new HIV infections may be among young people under the age of 25. In 1994, among people between the ages of 25 and 44, HIV-related illnesses caused

- *1 in every 3 deaths of African-American men*
- *1 in every 5 deaths of African-American women*

Although some men infected with HIV were unwilling or unable to report the source of their infection, the CDC did have some risk factors to report in 1997. Of HIV cases among boys and men from age 13 to 24,

- *53 percent were in young men who had had sex with men*
- *6 percent were in young men infected through IV drug use*
- *6 percent were in men who had had sex with men and injected drugs*
- *6 percent were in young men infected during sex with women*
- *2 percent were in hemophilia patients*

Some women infected with HIV were also unwilling or unable to report the source of their infection. But for girls and women ages 13 to 24, of all reported HIV cases up to 1997,

- *44 percent were in young women infected during sex with men*
- *12 percent were in young women infected through IV drug use*

In late 1997, WHO reported that more than 30.6 million people around the world were known to be infected with HIV. At the rate HIV is spreading, between 40 and 110 million people will be infected before the year 2000.

These are the deadly facts. There is no cure for AIDS. There is no vaccine to prevent HIV infection. Scientists don't expect to have a cure anytime soon.

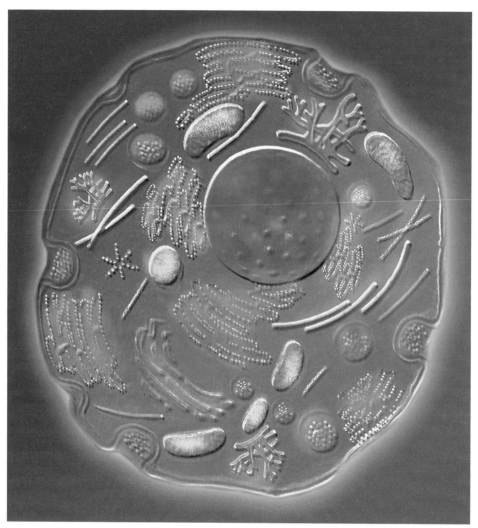

*A computer graphic of an animal cell: The big round structure
—the nucleus—carries the cell's genes. The oval yellow bodies—
mitochondria—provide energy. The folded, dotted structures—the
endoplasmic reticulum (ER)—carry ribosomes. Some of the round
bodies containing small particles—the vesicles—are expelling matter.
The golgi apparatus is the folded structure on the lower left.*

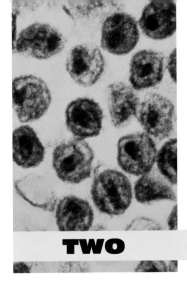

TWO

The Human Body–
Target for Infection

Cells, Cells, and More Cells

Cells are the real nitty-gritty stuff of life. Cells are the basic structural units that make up all living things. Some living creatures, such as amoebas and paramecia, are made of only a single cell. The average human body is composed of more than 100 trillion cells. We have skin cells, nerve cells, blood cells, bone cells, muscle cells, and brain cells, to name just a few. Each human being starts life as a single cell. This microscopic packet contains all the directions needed to produce a full-grown adult human.

Each cell is surrounded by a thin, transparent, and very strong membrane. The cell membrane protects and separates each cell from the rest of the world. The membrane controls everything that goes in and out of the cell.

Cells are like tiny factories. They need energy and food to survive and do their specific jobs. Each cellular package is filled with the machinery of life—structures called organelles. Membranes surround each of the organelles found inside the cell. The number and kinds of organelles in each cell depend on the cell's specific function.

The biggest, densest, and most distinct organelle in the cell is the nucleus. It functions as the cell's command center or headquarters. Inside the nucleus are the chromosomes—long twists of deoxyribonucleic acid. Deoxyribonucleic acid, or DNA, is life's master molecule. It can be thought of as a giant recipe book. Segments of chromosomes—genes—are the units of hereditary material that give directions for making new, exact copies of the cell. Contained in the genes are recipes for making every kind of protein that each one of the human body's 100 trillion cells needs to live.

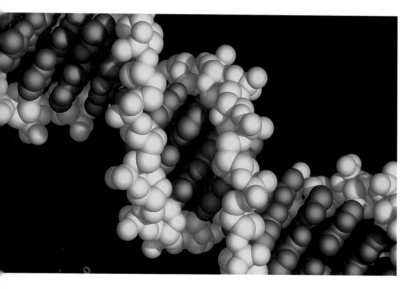

A computer model of a chromosome segment, a gene, shows the double-helix twist of DNA.

After the nucleus, the mitochondria are the largest organelles in the cell. Mitochondria are the cell's power plants. They convert the energy found in carbohydrates to adenosine triphosphate (ATP). ATP is like high-octane gasoline that is used to fuel all cellular processes. Some cells have more than a thousand mitochondria.

Cells also contain thousands or sometimes millions of tiny organelles called ribosomes. Each ribosome is less than one-millionth of an inch wide. Ribosomes are the cell's internal factories for producing protein molecules. Protein is the building material required for all life processes. Each protein molecule is made from a number of different amino acids arranged in a special order that is determined by the genetic code contained in the genes.

Another organelle, the endoplasmic reticulum (ER), is actually made up of many membranes. The ER could be considered the cell's internal plumbing. The ER membranes form a system of tubes and flattened sacs that are linked to the membrane surrounding the nucleus. Some of the ER membranes are smooth. Others are dotted with ribosomes. The ER stores and transports substances, mostly proteins made by the cell for use in other sections of the cell or outside the cell.

The Golgi apparatus is a system of membranelike sacs. It is considered the cell's packaging plant. Inside the sacs, the Golgi apparatus packages the protein molecules produced by the ribosomes into capsules. The capsules are sent to the cell's surface, where they fuse with the cell's outer membrane and release their contents. This is how cells secrete their hormones, enzymes, and other types of proteins into the blood stream when needed. Hormones and enzymes are proteins that speed up or slow down the chemical reactions of cells. Just as each organelle has its role in making each cell work smoothly, different groups of cells each help to keep the human body running.

The Body's Natural Defenses

Some of the 100 trillion cells in the human body make up what we call the immune system. To find a cure for AIDS, scientists need to learn precisely how HIV weakens and destroys the cells of the human body's immune system.

The immune system is the body's built-in police force against germs. Germs are microorganisms, or microbes. Microbes can come in the form of viruses, bacteria, fungi, parasites, or other tiny invaders that cause disease. The human body is warm and moist inside, a perfect home for viruses and other microbes. Some cells of the immune system are stationed near the body's natural openings: the mouth, the anus, the vagina, the eyes. But if microbes do make it past these guards, other cells of the immune system are designed to hunt them down and destroy them before they can multiply and cause infection.

Any organism that triggers the immune system into action is called an antigen. Antigens can be germs, or they can be bits and pieces of those germs. Cells or pieces of cells from other people also act as antigens because they do not carry marker molecules that say "self." This is why the body rejects skin or organ transplants, unless the help of drugs that turn off the immune system for a while is enlisted.

Under normal circumstances, the immune system functions as a personal physician that cures and protects us against the disease-causing microbes that are lurking nearby, just waiting for a chance to multiply and cause infection. But after being infected with HIV and the onset of AIDS, the body is left defenseless and unable to fight off infections.

The immune system itself is a complicated network of organs, tissues, cells, and chemical substances that circulate in the blood and lymph. Lymph is the clear fluid that flows between cells. Like the interconnected system of vessels and arteries that transport blood to all parts of the body, the lymph system is a complex system of vessels and passageways that carries lymph to all cells of the body.

The most important immune system cells are the white blood cells called lymphocytes. Lymphocytes are produced from stem cells, which are made in the bone marrow—spongy material found in the hollow areas inside bones. Some stem cells migrate to the thymus, a multi-lobed gland found in the lower part of the neck and upper part of the chest. Inside the thymus, the stem cells grow into lymphocytes called T cells.

A false-color electron micrograph—a colored, microscopic photo— shows the cortex of a thymus, where stem cells grow into the round T cells.

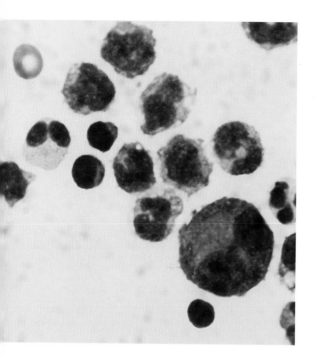 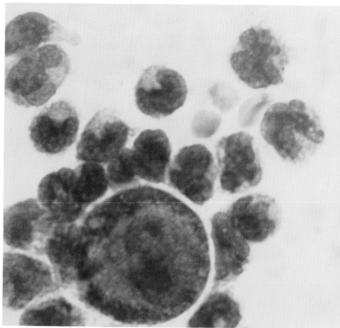

T cells have two major jobs. Some T cells act as helpers and cellular traffic cops. Other T cells work as killer cells that attack and destroy cells already infected by viruses or other invaders. They work by secreting powerful chemical messengers called cytokines. Cytokines attach themselves to target cells and mark them for destruction. The cytokines are signals to killer cells. Think of these chemicals as markers that sound the alarm: "Here is an enemy. Come and destroy it." Other cytokines serve as chemical calls for help. They might be saying: "We have a problem here. Send reinforcements quickly." When help arrives in the form of other immune system cells and chemicals, the helper T cells direct and regulate the attacks against the invaders.

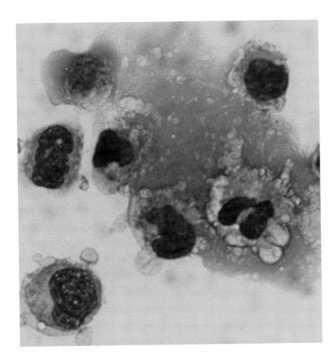

From left: *T cells encounter a large cancer cell. The T cells surround the cancer cell. And the cancer cell dissolves.*

Scientists can identify these helper T cells because they carry a special protein marker on their surfaces. The protein is called CD4. As a result, scientists call these helper cells CD4+ T cells, or T4 cells for short. These T4 cells are the favorite targets of HIV.

Other types of T cells have other kinds of protein markers. The T8 cell is another kind of lymphocyte that HIV can infect. T8 cells help the immune system recognize the body's own cells.

B cells are lymphocytes that mature either in the bone marrow itself or in glands other than the thymus. B cells make antibodies. Antibodies are protein molecules that keep a chemical record of previous fights with disease-causing viruses and bacteria. The Y-shaped antibody molecules are made to fit specific antigens much like a key fits into a lock. When antibodies lock onto an antigen, they serve as the flag that marks the invader for destruction by other cells of the immune system. Later, when a similar microbe invades again, the body recognizes it as an invader and the immune system cranks into action. The goal is to destroy the invading antigen or microbe before it can develop into a new infection. This is why most people get the measles, mumps, or chicken pox only one time. The immune system fought against these invading germs once. And it kept a chemical record to protect the body from contracting those illnesses again.

Each B cell is programmed to make only one kind of antibody. For example, one kind of B cell will make antibodies that attach to a virus that causes the flu. Another will produce antibodies that attach to particular rhinoviruses, a group of viruses that cause the common cold. Still another B cell might make antibodies that attach to bacteria that cause pneumonia. And so on. B cells produce antibodies against all kinds of viruses and bacteria.

The body can face millions of possible enemies, but it does not have room to store millions and millions of B cells to fight every possible invader. To solve this problem, the body makes and stores only a few of each kind of B cell. When an antigen appears and is identified, the matching B cells have the ability to multiply quickly. The cells become antibody factories. When called into action, they produce and pour millions of identical antibodies into the blood to fight the invading microbes.

T cells do not make antibodies, but they regulate the B cells' production of antibodies. Helper T cells increase antibody production.

Another important group of white cells are the phagocytes. Phagocyte means "cell eater." Phagocytes are very large cells that swallow and digest antigens. Monocytes—a type of phagocyte—circulate in the blood, looking for invaders to eat.

Macrophages are monocytes that move within the space between cells of the body, usually through the lymph system. Macrophage means "big eater." Macrophages are the body's garbage collectors. They surround worn-out cells, germs, and other debris floating in the blood and lymph, and then they digest them.

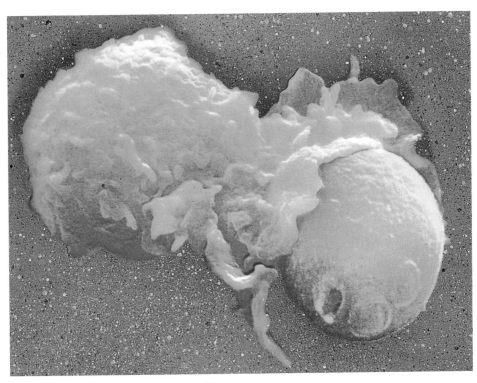

A macrophage eats a yeast cell.

The immune system has the ability to recognize millions of different enemies. The success of the immune system working against an invading microbe depends entirely on a complex and dynamic communication network between cells. Millions and millions of immune system cells are organized into sets and subsets. These groups of cells pass information back and forth. For example, T cells attract macrophages to an antigen, then the macrophages can gobble it up. The presence of macrophages, and maybe even the T cells themselves, also causes B cells to produce more antibodies.

Identifying Invaders

The immune system does much more than simply protect us from infection. Immune system cells work as scavengers or garbage collectors. They rid the body of worn-out cells, bits and pieces of dead cells, and other cellular debris floating in the blood or lymph vessels. The immune system helps control normal processes within the body as well. One of the most important functions of the system is its ability to tell the difference between the body's own cells and those belonging to invaders. In other words, immune system cells have the wonderful ability to distinguish between self and nonself.

Each cell in our body carries special marker molecules that advertise self. Think of a typical cell as being an orange covered with knobby toothpicks and colorful little marker flags. On a real cell, these toothpicks and flags are bits of protein and other special molecules. One or more of these bits of protein is a self marker that tells the immune system's hunter and killer cells that everything is fine. When certain immune defenders come across a cell or microbe that has no self marker, the alarm is sounded. The system swings into action to meet the threat of disease. In other situations, the immune system might mistake cells marked as self as being nonself. Such a mistake results in immune system cells attacking other good cells of the body. This type of problem is called an autoimmune disease.

When the immune system's ability to recognize self from nonself breaks down, the body produces T cells and antibodies that are directed against the body's own cells and organs. These misguided T cells and autoantibodies, as they are called, can cause a lot of damage. For example, T cells that attack pancreas cells contribute to diabetes. The autoantibody known as rheumatoid factor is common in people with rheumatoid arthritis, a very painful and crippling autoimmune disease. People with systemic lupus erythematosus, or lupus, have autoantibodies to many types of their own body's cells.

Sometimes the immune system overreacts and attacks harmless substances, such as pollen, dust, or animal hair, that get into our nose or eyes or enter through tiny cuts in the skin. The result is an allergy. Pollen and animal hair are a special kind of antigen called an allergen. An allergic reaction is a kind of false alarm. It is the result of the immune system working hard to get rid of an allergen.

When the immune system is weakened or shut down, the doors swing open for all kinds of disease-causing microbes that are just waiting for a chance to do their dirty work. Bacteria, parasites, and viruses swarm inside to cause infections that usually do not harm healthy people. Such infections are called "opportunistic." It is opportunistic infections that eventually kill a person with AIDS.

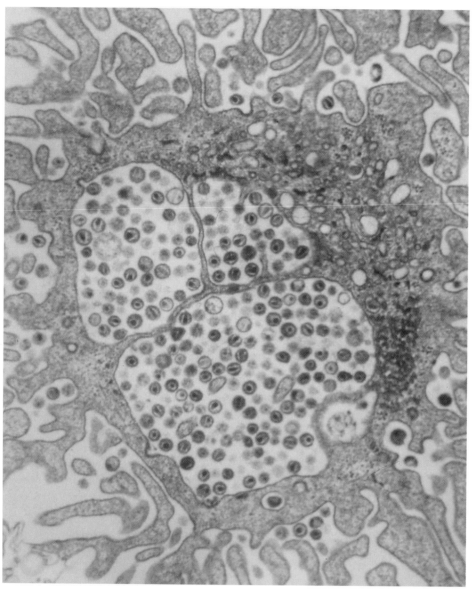

HIV particles fill a white blood cell. Like other viruses, HIV can only reproduce inside a cell.

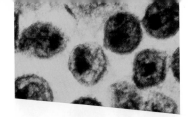

nd smallest living
d argue that a virus
is not alive at all. They   t in the gray world
somewhere between the living and the nonliving. A virus does
not need food to obtain energy. A virus does not need water. A
virus does not need to eliminate waste. So a virus is not really
"alive" in the sense that a bacterium or single-celled parasite
such as an amoeba is alive. And a virus is not alive in the same
sense that your pet dog or cat, or you or your friends, are alive.

But a virus can make new copies of itself. If a living organism
is defined as something that reproduces itself, then by that de-
finition, a virus is indeed alive. But a virus cannot reproduce by
itself, and it cannot reproduce outside of a cell. Each type of

virus can make new copies of itself only inside a specific kind of cell. Different viruses take different things from their host cells to complete the duplication process. Viruses are parasites of cells.

Viruses are the smallest microorganisms that we know of, existing in the submicroscopic world. To compare size, consider that most common bacteria are about 1 to 2 microns in diameter. A micron is one-millionth of a meter. Using the very best light microscope, the human eye can see particles as small as 0.2 to 1 micron in diameter. Viruses are much smaller. They are so small that powerful electron microscopes are needed just to see their outlines.

Viruses are super simple in structure. Almost all viruses are composed of only two parts: a coat of protein, which is wrapped around a core of nucleic acid. The nucleic acid core— a small piece of DNA—contains genetic information for making new copies of the virus. The core is surrounded and protected by a protein coat called the capsid. In some cases, the capsid is surrounded by a membranelike fatty envelope. The capsid and the envelope help the virus to survive during its time outside of a cell. Some viruses have very tough protective capsids. Other viruses are very fragile.

Viruses are DNA pirates. They must live inside other cells and steal those cells' ability to reproduce. Once inside a cell, the virus sheds its protein coat and plugs itself into the cell's own DNA. The naked strand of viral DNA becomes a genetic hijacker. It changes the cell's genetic instructions and turns the cell into a tiny virus factory that makes copy after copy of the virus.

Viruses must accomplish eight key steps to reproduce themselves inside a human cell.

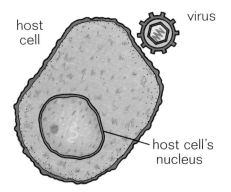

host cell

virus

1. *The virus attaches itself to the outside of the cell it will infect.*

host cell's nucleus

2. *The virus or its DNA penetrates the cell's thick protective membrane.*

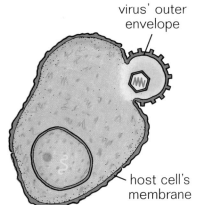

virus' outer envelope

host cell's membrane

viral protein coat

3. *The viral DNA sheds its coat, freeing the genetic material.*

host cell DNA

4. *Safely inside the cell, the viral DNA takes charge of the cell's reproductive machinery. The host cell reads or expresses the genetic functions coded by the virus.*

combination DNA

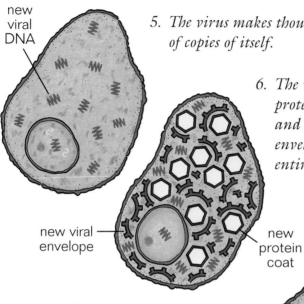

new viral DNA

5. *The virus makes thousands of copies of itself.*

6. *The virus makes new protein coats for itself, and sometimes new fatty envelopes to hold the entire structure together.*

new viral envelope

new protein coat

7. *The virus directs the cell to put all of these new parts together into new viral particles.*

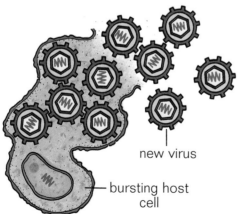

new virus

bursting host cell

8. *The worn-out cell dies and bursts open, spilling out thousands of fresh new viruses. Each new virus goes in search of another cell in which to start the cycle all over.*

What Is a Retrovirus?

A virus usually consists of a core made up of one or two strands of DNA surrounded by a protein coat. But in some instances, the genetic material inside the core is made of RNA, which is short for ribonucleic acid. Inside human cells, RNA transmits and translates instructions written in the genes. Viruses with RNA cores are called retroviruses. HIV is a retrovirus.

Information in the DNA molecule is written in a special code that consists of four chemical building blocks, called nucleotides. Each nucleotide is a piece of the code. Think of the different combinations of nucleotides as words, sentences, paragraphs, or entire volumes of information.

Inside human cells, DNA makes RNA, or ribonucleic acid, to send messages from the nucleus to other parts of the cell. RNA serves as both messenger and message. To send the message, a special chemical substance inside the cell reads a part of the DNA master program. The substance is an enzyme called transcriptase. Using the four basic nucleotides that make up the genetic code, transcriptase writes the message as a strand of RNA. This process is called transcription.

DNA always stays safely coiled inside the cell nucleus. But RNA messengers constantly travel around inside the cell, delivering messages to different pieces of a cell's internal machinery. The RNA messages carry instructions for building proteins and keeping the cell running smoothly.

A virus is a hijacker. Once inside a cell, the virus splices its genetic core directly into the DNA found inside the cell nucleus. It then proceeds to take over the transcription process. The virus writes new messages that tell the cell to make new copies of the viral core and proteins for new protective coats.

Retroviruses do things backwards. They are "retro" in the

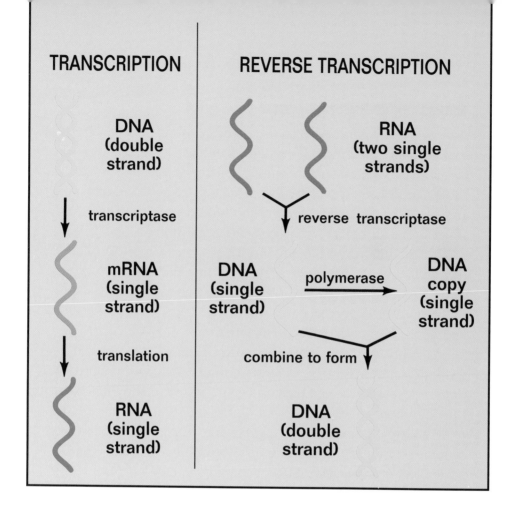

TRANSCRIPTION	REVERSE TRANSCRIPTION
DNA (double strand)	**RNA** (two single strands)
↓ transcriptase	↓ reverse transcriptase
mRNA (single strand)	**DNA** (single strand) → polymerase → **DNA copy** (single strand)
↓ translation	combine to form ↓
RNA (single strand)	**DNA** (double strand)

sense that they reverse life's usual drumbeat rhythm—cellular machinery turning DNA into RNA, and RNA into proteins. Instead, retroviruses change RNA into DNA, DNA into protein. Because their genetic core is made of RNA, retroviruses write their message backwards into the DNA of the host cell. This process is called reverse transcription. This backwards writing is done by an enzyme called reverse transcriptase. The greatest success to date in treating HIV infection has been the use of drugs that block the action of reverse transcriptase and the other steps in HIV's reproduction cycle.

Viruses, Disease, and Plague

The word "virus" comes from a Latin word for poison. Human contact with these tiny cellular parasites often has led to widespread and sometimes disastrous consequences. Over the past 2,000 years, smallpox killed millions of people in Europe and Asia. When Christopher Columbus and other European explorers traveled to North and South America, they brought smallpox and other viral diseases with them. Native Americans had no natural resistance to these new diseases. In the Americas, millions more people died from these diseases.

Viruses still infect people, make them sick, and sometimes kill them. Some viral diseases can be treated with medicines. Some cannot. Warts and the common cold are caused by viruses. Viruses also cause measles, mumps, chicken pox, polio, hepatitis, and yellow fever, as well as different kinds of influenza, the flu.

The single deadliest natural disaster of the twentieth century was not caused by a tornado, a volcano, an earthquake, or a hurricane. It was caused by a virus. Between 1918 and 1919, a worldwide epidemic of what was called Spanish flu killed between 20 million and 40 million people. The disease was spread around the world by soldiers fighting during World War I.

In 1997, scientists at the U.S. Armed Forces Institute of Pathology studied bits of lung tissue taken from the bodies of soldiers who died during the 1918 Spanish flu epidemic. With powerful microscopes, they looked at the viruses still contained in the tissue samples. Their work revealed that the Spanish flu was caused by an influenza virus that originated in American pigs. The findings support a theory that flu viruses from pigs are much more dangerous for humans than for pigs.

Experts believe that most flu viruses reside in the cells of birds. Occasionally, however, a virus from birds infects pigs. Like humans, all mammals have immune systems. Once infected, a pig's immune system attacks the virus. Over time, the virus must mutate, or change genetically, in order to survive. The result is a new virus that may be deadly to humans. Since the 1918 Spanish flu epidemic, two other flu viruses have spread all over the world—Asian flu in 1957 and Hong Kong flu in 1968. Both types of flu were caused by viruses that mutated in pigs. People died in both epidemics, but not in the huge numbers they had in the 1918 Spanish flu epidemic.

Disease Agents Too Small to See

Many of the most important discoveries in microbiology occurred in the 1800s. Although viruses had not been discovered yet, nineteenth-century scientists did know about

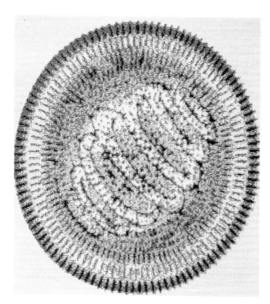

A computer graphic shows the influenza virus magnified about 200,000 times.

microbes like bacteria. The scientists debated two major questions. First, did microbes appear spontaneously in decaying matter, or were they the result of a self-duplication process?

The great French scientist Louis Pasteur solved the problem. He showed that any type of sterilized fluid would remain free of bacterial growth as long as bacteria carried in the air did not "infect" that fluid. Pasteur used special swan-necked flasks to prove his theory. The long curved neck of the flasks allowed air to reach the fluid, but not airborne bacteria. More than 140 years later, Pasteur's flasks, with their original contents, remain free of bacteria in the Pasteur Museum in Paris.

Pasteur's experiment was simple, but it had important consequences. Physicians began to understand the need for sterilizing surgical tools. Other medical and scientific research techniques changed as well. For example, scientists hoping to grow a single type of microbe, rather than a collection of many types, knew that they must start with a sterile growth medium.

The second huge question debated by nineteenth-century microbiologists was whether microbes caused specific diseases. If they did, how could one be sure which microbe was responsible? German scientist Robert Koch was one of many who decided to find out. Koch developed a set of rules to help distinguish between actual disease-causing agents, or pathogens, and microbes that were simply contaminants in a sample. For a microbe to be considered a disease-causing agent, Koch said it must meet the following criteria:

1. *The organism must be regularly found in the lesions or sores of a disease.*
2. *The organism must be isolated in sterile culture, completely free of other microbes.*

3. *Introducing a culture of pure organisms into a host should cause the disease.*
4. *The same organism should be found once again in the lesions of the new host.*

Koch proved his own postulates. He showed that the disease anthrax that infects cattle is caused by a specific bacterium. Scientists began using Koch's ideas to classify all kinds of bacteria and the diseases they caused.

By the 1890s, much had been learned about the microscopic world of bacteria. But the best microscopes available at the time could be used to see only bacteria whose size was at least 1 or 2 microns. And there were signs that there were even smaller microbes.

In 1886, scientists in several parts of the world were studying a disease of the tobacco plant called mosaic disease, which caused a pattern of light and dark areas on the plant's leaves. During experiment after experiment, the tobacco mosaic disease was transmitted from plant to plant. But no matter how closely the scientists looked, they could not find the microorganism responsible.

Special filters called Chamberland filter-candles were developed. The filters had pores that were much too small for bacteria to get through. In 1892, a young Russian scientist named Dimitrii Ivanovsky reported that tobacco mosaic disease remained infectious even after pure cultures were strained through the smallest Chamberland filters. Other scientists repeated the experiment. Tobacco mosaic virus was the first virus ever isolated by scientists.

By the 1930s, viruses were classified according to the host cell that they infected. There are three main groups of viruses:

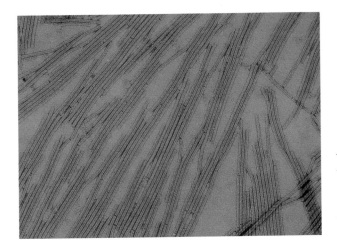

An electron micrograph shows the tobacco mosaic virus, magnified about 300,000 times.

plant cell viruses, animal cell viruses, and viruses that only infect bacteria. These viruses are called bacteriophage. During the last half of this century, scientists have learned much about what viruses are and how they live and reproduce. They not only classify viruses by the types of cells they infect, but also by the chemical composition of the virus, its shape, and its size. Many viruses satisfy Koch's postulates. Just like the bacteria that causes anthrax, viruses can reproduce and cause disease.

By the end of the twentieth-century, medical scientists thought that they were close to knowing everything about bacteria, viruses, and other causes of infectious disease. They've had some success. The smallpox virus exists only in test tubes kept frozen and locked away in Atlanta and Moscow. Polio has been all but wiped out. But other diseases that once were thought to be beaten are making deadly comebacks. Malaria is again killing thousands of people in tropical areas of the world. Tuberculosis is making a comeback. The flu never left. Bacteria, viruses, and parasites still cause about half of all human deaths.

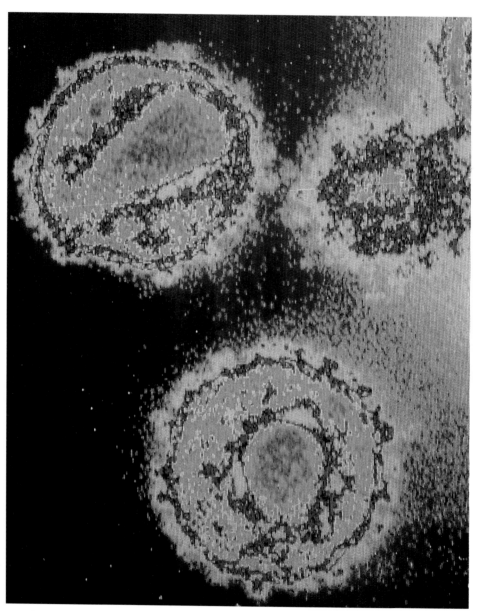

HIV, the virus that causes AIDS

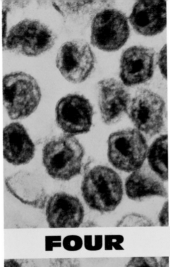

FOUR

Catching AIDS

How HIV Infects Human Cells

Viruses and retroviruses come in variations of two basic shapes. They can be a helix that looks like a squat column. Or they can look like knobby soccer balls covered with spikes. HIV is one of the knobby soccer balls. It is very small, even within the ultra-small world of viruses. Consider that HIV is only 10,000 nucleotides long. Some viruses are even smaller. The parvovirus—less than 2,000 nucleotides long—is a single strand of DNA. Still, inside the human body, parvovirus can cause a rash, fever, and temporary arthritis. But most viruses are larger than HIV. The smallpox virus, which once killed millions of people throughout the world, is 180,000 nucleotides in size.

HIV's outer envelope contains two important protein molecules, gp120 and gp41. The gp120 molecule allows HIV to attach to the human immune system's T4 cells. T4 cells have protein receptor sites on their outside membranes made with a

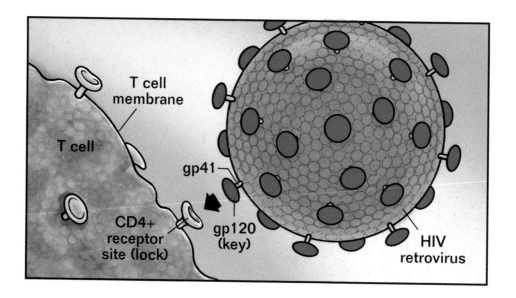

molecule called CD4+. Think of each CD4+ site as a lock. The gp120 molecule is the key that gives HIV access to the cell. The gp41 molecule allows HIV's outside envelope to fuse with the host-cell membrane. The HIV coat is lined with another protein called p17. Once HIV completes its deadly hijacking of a host cell's internal reproduction machinery, p17 will form the outer coat of new HIV particles.

HIV's core is surrounded by a membrane made of three more proteins. Scientists call them p24, p6, and p7. In addition to the two strands of RNA, the core contains a variety of enzymes. The virus uses the enzymes—including reverse transcriptase, RNAse, polymerase, integrase, and protease—to take over the host cell. These enzymes are the targets of researchers. If scientists can find a way to disrupt HIV's normal life cycle, AIDS might be prevented or at least slowed down.

HIV's life cycle is a series of eight stages.

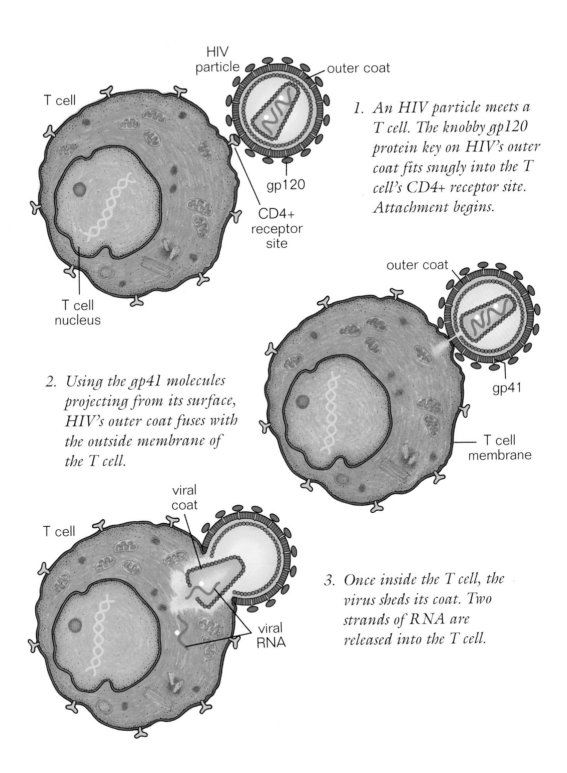

HIV particle

outer coat

T cell

gp120

CD4+ receptor site

T cell nucleus

1. *An HIV particle meets a T cell. The knobby gp120 protein key on HIV's outer coat fits snugly into the T cell's CD4+ receptor site. Attachment begins.*

outer coat

gp41

T cell membrane

2. *Using the gp41 molecules projecting from its surface, HIV's outer coat fuses with the outside membrane of the T cell.*

viral coat

T cell

viral RNA

3. *Once inside the T cell, the virus sheds its coat. Two strands of RNA are released into the T cell.*

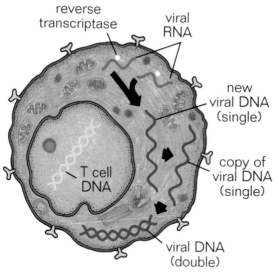

reverse transcriptase

viral RNA

new viral DNA (single)

copy of viral DNA (single)

T cell DNA

viral DNA (double)

4. *Reverse transcriptase copies a single strand of DNA from the two strands of viral RNA. RNAse chops off the old RNA from the DNA copy. Then polymerase makes another exact copy of the new viral DNA and links the strands of DNA.*

5. *The brand-new double strand of viral DNA moves into the nucleus of the T cell. Once inside, integrase fuses the viral DNA with the T cell's DNA. Hijacking is complete.*

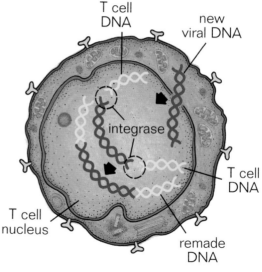

T cell DNA

new viral DNA

integrase

T cell DNA

T cell nucleus

remade DNA

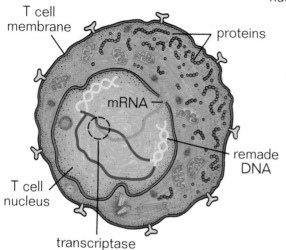

T cell membrane

proteins

mRNA

remade DNA

T cell nucleus

transcriptase

6. *The remade DNA begins issuing orders for the production of proteins necessary to build new HIV particles. Using instructions in the form of messenger RNA and transfer RNA, ribosomes in the T cell begin assembling amino acids into large, inactive proteins. These proteins move to the cell membrane.*

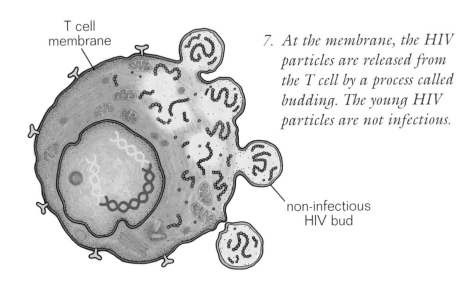

T cell
membrane

7. *At the membrane, the HIV
particles are released from
the T cell by a process called
budding. The young HIV
particles are not infectious.*

non-infectious
HIV bud

non-infectious
HIV particle

enzyme and
protein rich
cytoplasm

8. *Protease molecules split
the large proteins inside
the HIV particle into a
bunch of smaller proteins
and enzymes. With that,
the HIV particle is a ma-
ture, infectious retrovirus.*

infectious HIV
particle

These T cells are infected with HIV.

The genetic recipe for HIV comes in the form of a single strand of RNA. Using the internal machinery and materials of the T cell, this RNA strand produces a double strand of DNA. The new deadly DNA works its way into the T cell's DNA. Once there, it waits. And waits. And waits.

HIV is not dormant during the time it waits. It slowly reproduces itself inside the T cell. Years go by. But HIV eventually reappears with a horrible fury. Researchers are still unclear as to what triggers HIV to reproduce at great speed and burst forth from T cells in massive numbers of new viral particles. The result of HIV's massive reappearance is the disease we know as AIDS. Billions of new viruses infect new host cells. The immune system is not able to keep up the fight. With defenses weakened, the body is not able to fight off other disease-causing bacteria and viruses. That is why AIDS victims often suffer from many different kinds of rare infections at the same time.

Internal Mechanics of Transmission

The first cells to encounter HIV are most likely the macrophages. Macrophages are the cell eaters that roam through the blood and lymph looking for invading bacteria, viruses, fungi, parasites, old worn-out cells, or other bits of debris to surround and digest. These all-purpose garbage collectors can be found in large numbers behind the thin, moist linings of the anus and cervix. The linings of these areas are only a single cell in thickness. They are easy points of entry for viruses, bacteria, and other invaders. Just a tiny nick or cut opens a doorway into the body. In comparison, the linings of the vagina, lungs, nose, and mouth are much thicker. Covered with a thick, sticky substance called mucus, these many-cells-thick linings provide much tougher obstacles for microbes looking for a way inside the human body.

When HIV does find a way inside the body, most likely a macrophage recognizes it as an invader and gobbles it up. But the macrophage can't digest HIV like it digests other viruses. HIV is still functioning. And once HIV is inside a cell of the immune system, it cannot be detected by other immune-system killer cells. The macrophage becomes an unwitting taxi that takes HIV even deeper inside the body.

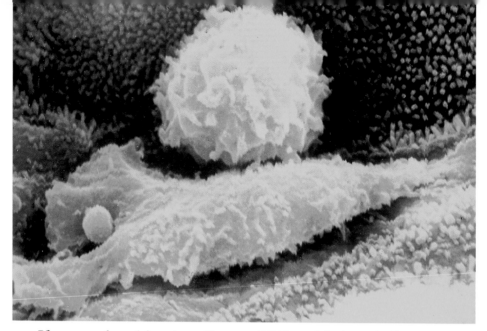

If a macrophage (above) *swallows an HIV particle, it can't digest it like it digests other viruses. HIV lives to reproduce and infect and kill other cells of the immune system.*

The HIV-infected macrophage goes about its work. Eventually, it makes its way to a lymph node, a gathering point for all kinds of immune-system cells. The infected macrophage has brought the enemy smack into the middle of immune-system headquarters. At the lymph node, T4 cells rush in to help B cells and other killer cells fight the virus gathered by the macrophage. The T4 cells link to the surface of the macrophage. At this point, HIV moves into the T4 cells. The T cells become infected.

Soon after a person is infected with HIV, the virus begins to make new copies of itself by the millions. The first outward signs are flulike: fever, a dry cough, diarrhea, shaking chills or night sweats, and swollen glands in the neck, armpits, or groin. These swollen glands are the lymph nodes, the spot where HIV is busily building new viruses. But after this first round of illness, HIV seems to rest or go into hiding.

Out of Sight

During the past few years, medical scientists have been studying people known to be infected with HIV but who show no outward symptoms of AIDS. These people appear healthy. They feel healthy. But they are not healthy.

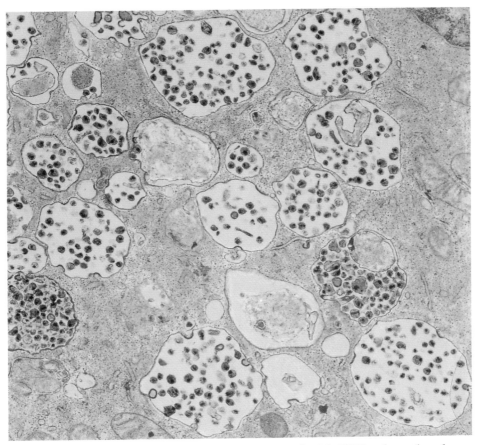

A false-color micrograph of a T4 cell infected with HIV—the red and green dots in the yellow vesicles—shows the buildup of HIV within a T cell.

As expected, scientists find little evidence of the virus in the blood of people who show no AIDS symptoms. But the lymphoid tissue contains huge amounts of HIV. There is other evidence that the virus is reproducing rapidly. Findings suggest that the virus not only hides out in the lymph nodes and other organs of the lymphatic system, but reproduces there as well. These organs include the spleen, as well as the tonsils and adenoids, spongy lumps of tissue found at the back of the throat.

Think of the lymph nodes and other lymphoid organs as sticky nets. These nets are designed to trap broken old cells, dead cells, or bacteria and viruses that have been attacked and killed by the immune system. HIV circulating in the blood is trapped by the cells in these nets. These catcher cells are called follicular dendritic cells. For a long time, scientists relied on blood tests to show that HIV was present in the body. They were confused when they had sick people with no sign of HIV in their blood. They now know that the catcher cells inside the lymph nodes clear HIV from the blood. In doing their job, these catcher cells actually help HIV to build up into huge numbers.

In the case of other viruses, such a concentration makes the job of the immune system's killer cells much easier to complete. The killer cells converge on the concentration of viruses in the lymph nodes and wipe them out. But because HIV infects the cells of the immune system, the concentration of virus becomes a convenient means of infecting new cells. In essence, the virus is building up a huge stockpile of itself even when the infected person appears to be healthy. This period can last for years.

During the time when HIV appears to be dormant, the virus can also be hiding and reproducing inside the brain. The virus is carried into the brain by macrophages. Because macrophages are cells of the immune system, they are recognized as self. As a result, these infected cells can pass through the barrier that protects brain cells from bacteria and other disease-causing agents. HIV is hidden undetected inside the macrophages, much like Greek soldiers hid inside a giant wooden horse to enter the gates of Troy.

Once inside the brain, HIV doesn't infect nerve cells. Instead, it causes them to wither and die. Scientists are not sure why. The brain slowly wastes away and actually shrinks in size. As a result, many AIDS victims suffer mental conditions that leave them unable to move or think clearly and unable to recognize loved ones. Autopsies of people who have died from AIDS reveal brains that look much different from the brains of healthy people. The brains of some AIDS victims have shrunk in size by 20 percent.

Other changes occur during the time when HIV appears to be dormant. HIV may activate T4 cells to work harder. Some scientists think the virus causes the cells to work themselves to death. Others think that HIV flips a genetic switch that programs the T4 cells to commit suicide. This programmed cell death is called apoptosis. Under normal circumstances, apoptosis is the body's method for regulating the number of the body's cells, including the immune system cells. HIV turns on the T4 cells' apoptosis and lets it run out of control.

As time goes on, more and more of the follicular dendritic cells that form the lymphatic organs die or become damaged. They are not replaced. So the body's ability to snare free-floating HIV from the blood is hampered. The virus begins to spill out into the blood in huge numbers, and it infects new immune system cells by the billions. The number of T4 cells in the blood drops dangerously. The body begins to suffer from all kinds of opportunistic infections. The immune system fighters are dead. There is nothing to stop HIV's spread, and the onset of infections known as AIDS begins. HIV has opened the door to all kinds of disease-causing microorganisms.

Scientists have changed the way they think about AIDS. The process was thought to be initial infection, then a long period of rest, then explosive infection and death. But it seems that the disease never truly rests at all. All along, it is quietly making billions of copies of itself while it hides inside the very cells that are supposed to hunt it down and destroy it.

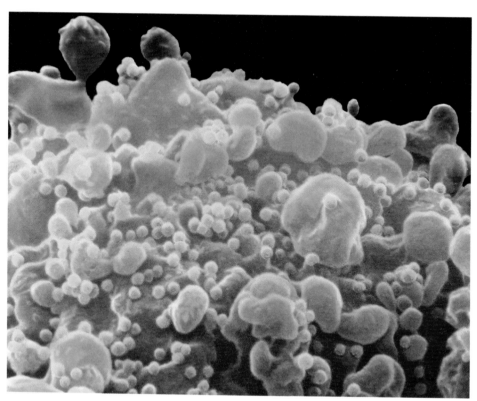

False-colored yellow HIV particles bud from a pink T cell.

Because of this information, doctors have changed the way they treat people infected with HIV. In the past, doctors treated HIV-infected people when some outward sign of deterioration or sickness appeared. They relied totally on the number of T cells seen in blood tests. When that number dropped below 500 T cells per cubic milliliter of blood, they would begin heavy treatment with antiviral drugs. But it appears that is already too late.

Different Strains of HIV

HIV reproduces quickly and sloppily. The virus is sloppy in that it produces mutated forms of itself in large numbers. These mutant forms may have one or two slight differences. The differences might appear in HIV's protein coat or in its reverse transcriptase. This ability to mutate rapidly becomes important when scientists start looking for drugs that can stop HIV.

Earlier treatment might help. But there are other problems. Early treatment with powerful AIDS drugs can make the virus resistant to those drugs later on. The virus mutates quickly, changing its genetic makeup. As the virus copies itself, the protein markers studding its outside surface change slightly. With the binding sites changed, the drugs cannot attach to the virus. In a sense, the virus has changed its locks. Keys used by the drugs no longer work. As a result, the virus outwits these chemical attacks in a matter of months. The drugs become useless.

There are several known strains of HIV. Some have been named. The two best known strains are HIV-1 and HIV-2. HIV-1 was the virus first discovered in the United States, Europe, and Africa. HIV-2 was discovered in central Africa a few years later. In late 1994, a study of prostitutes living in several central African countries provided researchers with evidence that HIV-2 causes AIDS much less quickly than its cousin, HIV-1, the strain found in the United States. If scientists can find the actual structural or genetic reason why HIV-2 is different, they might be able to use that knowledge to slow down the life cycle and the destruction of the immune system caused by HIV-1.

Because HIV mutates at a high rate, it is possible that more new strains of the virus could develop. While it is possible that new strains of HIV might not cause disease in people, it is more likely that they could cause even more trouble. New strains of HIV might be impossible to detect. They also could infect different types of cells. They could even be transmitted in different ways, such as through the air.

Think about the flu virus for a moment. Every year, new strains of this rhinovirus arrive to cause disease and, in some cases, death. In the United States alone, thousands of people die every year from the flu and flu-related pneumonia. More than 20,000 died from flu-related problems in 1992. Results from current research indicate that HIV mutates at a rate five times faster than the influenza virus. HIV has the potential to develop many more new strains and cause all kinds of terrible problems in the future.

Gaps in Knowledge

Many large gaps in knowledge about AIDS still exist. One of the most vexing problems facing researchers is defining exactly how HIV causes the immune system to collapse. Such information is essential to scientists working toward a cure for AIDS.

The question is basic, but finding the answer has not been easy. Scientists know that people infected with HIV have a much lower number of T4 cells. But no one can yet agree on exactly how HIV leads to the destruction of these important cells. There are many theories. Some scientists think that the virus itself may directly kill the T4 cells—HIV might somehow cause T4 cells to implode or burst. Or the virus could cause infected T cells to fuse together into large clumps. Large clumps of T cells could be recognized as "foreign." As a result, they would be attacked by other killer cells. Scientists have shown that HIV does both of these things to immune system cells in the laboratory. But exactly how it does these things still is not known.

During studies with hundreds of infected patients, scientists could detect little or no HIV present in the bloodstream when killing damage was occurring to the T4 cells. It may be that those early tests simply were not sensitive enough to detect the HIV. Researchers using newer, more precise techniques are finding that the amount of virus hiding in the cells of infected people is much higher than previously thought. This is because HIV is busy making billions of copies of itself while safely hiding in the lymph nodes, the brain, and other organs.

Other scientists think that HIV somehow sends a message to other portions of the immune system, especially the killer cells. This message causes the killer cells to go haywire and kill uninfected T4 cells. Still other researchers think that HIV triggers the cells of the immune system to commit suicide by apoptosis. No one knows which, if any, of these theories is correct.

Using a condom is one way to prevent the spread of AIDS.

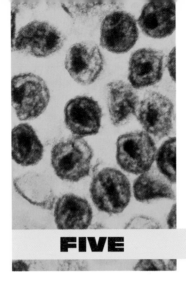

FIVE

Preventing the Spread of AIDS

How HIV Spreads from Person to Person

Before HIV can cause any damage at all, it must get inside a human body. In order for that to happen, HIV must travel from the inside of an infected person to the inside of another person.

Many viruses spread easily from person to person. This is the case with the viruses that cause the flu or colds. These viruses live in the mucous membranes that line the lungs, throat, and sinuses. When you cough or sneeze, you spray large numbers of living viruses into the air. The viruses are found in sputum—the liquid droplets you expel into a handkerchief or onto your hand or into the air when you cough or sneeze. If you touch another person soon afterward, or if another person breathes in some of those droplets, the virus can infect him or her.

HIV is very different. The T4 cells of the immune system, in which HIV lives, are found in the bloodstream and other body fluids. In addition to blood, fluids that contain T4 cells include semen, secretions from the vagina and cervix, saliva, tears, mother's milk, urine, and feces. HIV has been found in all of these substances in infected people. In theory, each of these substances is capable of transmitting the virus to other people. Once outside the body, the HIV within any of these substances remains infectious until the liquid in the substance dries up.

HIV must stay moist to survive. Scientists know that HIV can survive in solutions of blood and water kept at room temperature for up to two weeks. And if blood is kept cool in a refrigerator, HIV can survive indefinitely.

The concentration of HIV in a particular fluid must be very high for the risk of infection to be high. The concentrations of HIV are usually the highest in the blood, semen, and vaginal secretions of infected people. For this reason, HIV is spread most easily from one person to another in four ways:

1. *During unprotected anal or vaginal intercourse.*
2. *Through the sharing of needles and syringes used for shooting drugs or steroids directly into the bloodstream.*
3. *From a mother to her unborn child.*
4. *By transfusions with contaminated blood products.*

HIV is not spread by casual contact. The virus is not spread by eating with, touching, or just being near someone who is infected with the virus or who has AIDS.

There have been a few documented cases where HIV was transmitted by oral sex, but such transmission is rare. And no one has been able to show without a doubt even one case

Unprotected intercourse (right) *and sharing needles* (below) *are two ways AIDS is spread from person to person.*

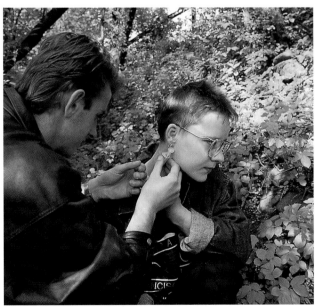

where HIV was transmitted in saliva. There are no known cases of kissing as a method of transmission. The concentration of HIV in saliva appears to be too low to cause infection. And there is no scientific evidence that HIV can be transmitted by mosquitoes or any other type of insect.

But many people have become infected with HIV through transfusions of contaminated blood products. In 1985, the U.S. government moved to protect the blood supply. Scientists developed tests to detect antibodies to HIV in blood. These tests are used to screen all blood products provided by blood donor services. The blood supply in the United States is much safer than it was in the mid-1980s. In 1994, the government estimated that only 1 in every 100,000 units of blood might have been infected with HIV. The risk has continued to decrease each year. To be 100 percent safe, however, people planning to have surgery should ask their doctor if they can donate their own blood in advance in case a transfusion is needed. It is important to remember that you cannot get AIDS from donating blood, because the instruments used are sterilized.

At Risk for Catching HIV

Like any disease, simply being exposed to the virus that causes AIDS does not mean you will catch it. But who wants to take the risk when the result can be death? Public health officials say that people most at risk for HIV infection include:

- *People with many sexual partners, especially those who engage in anal or vaginal intercourse without a condom. During anal intercourse, a male's penis is inserted into the anus of another person. During vaginal intercourse, a male's penis is inserted into a female's vagina.*

- *People who have shared intravenous needles any time since the late 1970s.*
- *Infants born to infected mothers.*

Protecting yourself from getting AIDS is actually quite easy. Not having sex and not injecting drugs provides almost 100 percent protection from becoming infected with HIV.

In the real world, however, totally abstaining from having sex might be difficult. Still, there are other ways to reduce your risk of becoming infected with HIV. For example, use a condom until you and your partner have been tested for HIV. Remember that HIV antibodies generally do not reach detectable levels until one to three, or even six, months following infection. If results come back negative—meaning that no antibodies to HIV were found in your blood—maintain a mutually faithful sexual relationship. If, however, you or your sexual partner have had sexual relations with other people, or you have not always been faithful to each other, you should protect yourselves in the following ways:

- *Do not engage in unprotected anal or vaginal intercourse. Protect yourself and your partner by using latex condoms. Proper use of condoms greatly reduces the chance of giving or getting infections, including HIV.*
- *Limit the number of your sexual partners. The more people you share sexual relations with, the greater your risk of getting a sexually transmitted disease, including HIV.*
- *Do not have sex, period, with people in the high-risk groups. These include people who use injectable drugs, prostitutes, men or women who have had many sexual partners, and men who have had unprotected anal sex with other men.*

Despite all of the good and helpful information about how to protect oneself from becoming infected with the AIDS virus, some people never get the message or choose to ignore it. As a result, AIDS continues to spread. But it no longer spreads silently. Physicians and scientists do have ways to detect the presence of HIV in the body, even before any symptoms of disease begin to appear.

Identifying the Presence of HIV

There are several laboratory blood tests being used to identify HIV infection. These tests identify the presence of antibodies to HIV present in the bloodstream. They do not detect HIV itself. Scientists now know that it takes about 14 weeks before HIV antibodies develop to levels in the bloodstream that are detectable using the tests.

The most common blood test in use today is called ELISA.

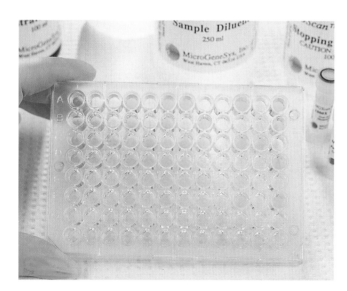

A positive reading in the ELISA test is determined by the amount of yellow color in individual wells.

ELISA is short for enzyme-linked immunoabsorbant assay. The ELISA test is very sensitive in identifying specific kinds of antibodies made by the immune system. It can detect very tiny amounts of antibodies in the blood. The ELISA test reveals the presence of antibodies that immune system cells make specifically to attach to parts of HIV's protective protein coat.

Because the ELISA test is so sensitive, it can be fooled by the presence of proteins and antibodies not at all related to HIV. For this reason, doctors use a second test to confirm the results of all positive ELISA tests.

The second test is known as the Western blot. This test is expensive and difficult to perform. That is why Western blot tests are used only to confirm the results of blood samples that tested positive using ELISA. The Western blot test is very specific. But it requires a trained technician to read the results, as errors in interpreting the results are possible. Even though

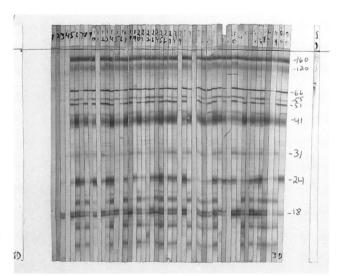

A positive reading in the Western blot test is determined by a line at two of three positions—lines 160, 41, or 24.

these blood tests are not 100 percent accurate, they are all that is available.

If you were tested for HIV infection and your test was negative, no antibodies to HIV were found in your blood. But it is important to remember that it may take three months or longer for a person to develop antibodies after getting infected with the AIDS virus. It is possible for a person to have HIV infection and test negative. For this reason, doctors recommend that people who engage in high-risk behavior should consider being retested every three months for up to one year after the first negative test, or after each episode of high-risk behavior.

What Being HIV-Positive Really Means

A positive antibody test means that the blood sample tested positive twice on the ELISA test and positive again on the Western blot test. Such a result generally means that the person is infected with HIV. It does not necessarily mean that the person has AIDS or will develop AIDS anytime soon. Current statistics indicate that more than half of all people infected with HIV develop AIDS within 10 years. And people with AIDS eventually die from AIDS-related disease, some much more quickly than others.

Throughout the United States, there are now sites that conduct anonymous, confidential testing for HIV infection. Anonymous testing means that you do not have to give your name to be tested. Confidential testing means that any information you provide at the testing site is protected by law. The laws protecting patient confidentiality vary from state to state. If you want more information about free HIV testing or counseling available in your area, it is a good idea to start by asking your doctor or calling your city, county, or state health department. You can also get information about testing sites by calling the following hotlines:

- *National AIDS Hotline: 1-800-342-AIDS or 1-800-342-2437 (staffed 24 hours a day)*
- *SIDA Hotline (Spanish language): 1-800-344-SIDA or 1-800-344-7432*
- *TTY/TTD AIDS Hotline: 1-800-243-7889 (for the hearing impaired)*
- *National STD (sexually transmitted diseases) Hotline: 1-800-227-8922*

The Symptoms of AIDS

Many people infected with HIV feel perfectly healthy. They often show no signs of illness. But their bodies are vulnerable to many other diseases and conditions. These diseases are called opportunistic or secondary infections. Some of these infections are caused by viruses, bacteria, fungi, parasites, and other types of microorganisms that may have been present in the body for a long time before the body became infected with HIV. But once the body's immune system has been damaged by HIV infection, the door to all kinds of other infections is wide open.

The actual physical symptoms of HIV infection are similar to those of many other common illnesses. But with HIV infection, the symptoms last longer and come back repeatedly. Some of the physical signs include:

- *A thick, whitish coating on the tongue or in the throat, and difficulty swallowing*
- *Fever, shaking chills, or night sweats*
- *Swollen glands in the neck, armpits, or groin*

- *Rapid weight loss of more than 10–15 pounds*
- *Constant diarrhea*
- *A dry, hacking cough, often accompanied by a shortness of breath*
- *Pink or purple flat or raised blotches that occur on or under the skin or inside the mouth, nose, eyelids, or rectum*

People with AIDS develop a large number of secondary infections. Some of the most common opportunistic infections are Pneumocystis carinii pneumonia, Kaposi's sarcoma, cryptosporidiosis, thrush, and herpes.

Pneumocystis carinii pneumonia (PCP) is caused by a microscopic, funguslike parasite that is thought to infect most humans during childhood. The organism normally remains dormant. But it is the leading cause of death in people with AIDS. This disease often is the first infection to appear in people infected with HIV. As a result, PCP is one of the diseases doctors use to establish the diagnosis of AIDS.

People with PCP develop a dry, hacking cough and shortness of breath. For weeks and even months before breathing problems occur, some people experience fever, fatigue, and weight loss. As PCP progresses to its most advanced form, the person's lungs become clogged. The lungs are not able to efficiently transport oxygen from inhaled air into the blood. Without oxygen in the blood, a person slowly suffocates and dies.

Kaposi's sarcoma is a rare but deadly type of skin cancer. In AIDS patients, the disease first appears as pink, purple, or brown lesions on the arms and legs. These wounds spread all over the body, inside and outside.

Cryptosporidiosis is a major cause of diarrheal illness in humans around the world. The disease is caused by a one-celled

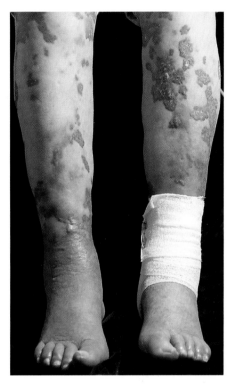

Lesions from Kaposi's sarcoma on an eye (below) *and legs* (right) *on AIDS patients*

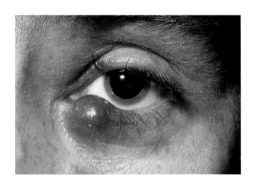

parasite that lives in cattle and domestic animals. The parasite is spread from animals to people through contact with animal feces, or by contaminated water or food. In people with normal immune systems, the parasite causes severe diarrhea and flulike intestinal problems that go away after a week or more without treatment. But in people with AIDS, the disease can last for months. Eventually, the loss of fluids can be massive enough to cause death.

One of the most common fungal infections in people with AIDS is thrush, or candidiasis. The disease is caused by the organism *Candida albicans.* The fungus is commonly found on the skin, and in the mouth, vagina, and intestinal tract of humans. In AIDS patients, the infection usually appears as white spots or patches on the sides of the tongue and inside the cheeks. The patches also can appear around the nails of fingers and toes, and on the skin around the armpits, groin, and rectum. Candidiasis is often the first visible sign of HIV infection.

Different forms of herpes virus infections also are common to people with AIDS. Cold sores appear on the lips, mouth, and genitals. Ulcers also can form on the skin, in the eyes, or near the anus.

The list goes on and on. Other diseases common to people with AIDS include toxoplasmosis, cryptococcosis, herpes zoster infections, also known as shingles, mycobacterium infection,

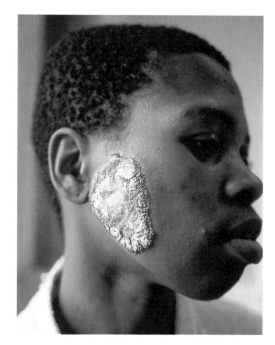

An ulcerated tuberculous lesion on the face of an AIDS patient

Epstein-Barr infection, cytomegalovirus infection, and tuberculosis. Although people with healthy immune systems can contract these diseases, their bodies have a much better chance of successfully fighting them off. But all of these infections are horrible causes of death for people infected with HIV.

Looking Ahead

Some people tend to place physicians and scientists on a type of philosophical pedestal. "No need to worry," they think. "Science and technology will save the day and find an answer quickly." But physicians and scientists are the first to say that they do not have all the answers. And the answers may not be found anytime soon. In the immediate future, we cannot look forward to any kind of magic pill or vaccine that will save us from the disease. Progress is being made in the treatment of AIDS and the search for a cure. But it is very slow progress. Unfortunately, there is still room for future disappointments, and even for reverses.

Nearly two decades after AIDS was first described in the United States, the epidemic has continued to expand throughout the world. In late 1997, the World Health Organization estimated that more than 29.5 million young people and adults had already been infected with HIV, the majority through heterosexual intercourse. Another 1.1 million infants were infected while still in their mothers' wombs. The numbers continue to rise in all categories. AIDS threatens to explode among the populations of Africa, India, China, and Southeast Asia, where more than half the people on earth live. The disease continues to spread, despite the fact that scientists now know more about HIV than about any other virus in the history of medical science.

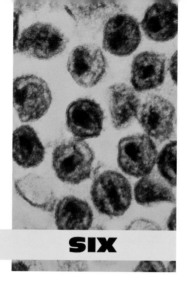

SIX

The Search for a Cure

Providing the Body with a Chemical Assist

Though billions of dollars have been spent on research, there still is nothing on the horizon that even remotely resembles a cure for AIDS. And there is nothing at all close to an effective vaccine against the disease.

A cure seems no closer than it did in 1981. Much of the newest information undermines previous assumptions about the virus. What many scientists thought they knew with certainty and confidence often has been thrown out the window.

Science is a very slow, painstaking process. Setbacks occur with much more regularity than breakthroughs. Scientists learn as much from what does not work as from what does work. Easy cures and quick answers are rare; they are not the normal result of real-world scientific research.

In 1996, however, researchers started to show the first real glimmer of optimism. More than 15,000 people from 125 countries gathered in Vancouver for the eleventh annual International Conference on AIDS. The key discovery discussed in Vancouver centered on the power of combining many different kinds of AIDS medicines. Used alone, none of the drugs is very effective. When combined in a type of chemical cocktail, however, the drugs appear to slow and even stop HIV from reproducing. Most AIDS drugs are designed to disrupt one or more of the complex steps HIV must complete to reproduce itself inside a host cell. Gum up enough of the process, the theory says, and the virus cannot reproduce at all. The newest drugs are called protease inhibitors. These drugs work by interrupting HIV's ability to reproduce itself at a specific point in its life cycle. Think of them as materials that clog up HIV's reproductive machinery. While not a cure, when combined with drugs that block the effectiveness of reverse transcriptase in HIV, protease inhibitors at least provide a means to improve and prolong the lives of people infected with HIV.

The Development of Anti-HIV Drugs

Nearly all approved drugs used by physicians to fight infections were discovered in the same way. Scientists randomly screen thousands of compounds every year. Some are human made, some are naturally occurring compounds found in plants, animals, and insects. At the National Cancer Institute (NCI), more than 12,000 natural products and compounds made in the laboratory are screened for anti-HIV activity every year.

When the AIDS virus was first isolated, it did not take long for researchers to find drugs that were very good at killing HIV. But there was a catch. These drugs were killing HIV in test tubes within the controlled surroundings of a laboratory, not inside the complex workings of a human body. About 1 of every 50 compounds tested by the NCI each year shows some ability to kill HIV. Many of those compounds that kill HIV in screening tests, however, also cause serious damage to human cells. Scientists know that the exposed virus is easy to kill. When HIV is tucked safely inside a T4 cell or other type of host cell, however, powerful drugs would kill the host cells as well as the virus. Some of these compounds can be modified and retested. Only the compounds that kill HIV while causing little or no damage to infected cells are candidates for development into drugs for human use.

The normal scientific procedure for testing the effectiveness of new drugs against disease in human beings can take many years to complete. In the United States, strong pressure was exerted by politicians and other groups to find drugs or treatments that would provide some type of quick help for AIDS patients. As a result, some new drugs were rushed past the normal testing procedures and into actual trials with sick people.

AZT was first tried on infected humans in 1985. AZT is a reverse transcriptase inhibitor. It blocks HIV from infecting new T4 cells. But the drug does not stop the reproduction of the virus inside already infected cells. Early results were promising enough that AZT was rushed onto the market.

That early hope for a quick cure has long since faded. In the United States, physicians use five different reverse transcriptase inhibiting drugs. The common names of these drugs are AZT, ddI, ddC, d4T, and 3TC. The drugs do work, for a while. Used by themselves, or even in combination, the benefits of reverse transcriptase inhibitors often are gone within a year. The AIDS virus mutates quickly into new forms that are resistant to the drugs' action, much as insects can become resistant to different types of pesticides.

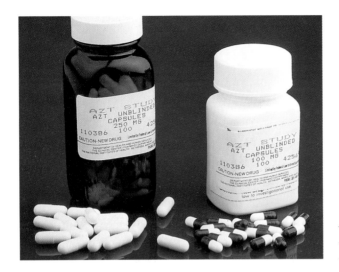

AZT was one of the first drugs used to fight HIV.

Drug resistance is becoming a problem for other virus-caused diseases as well as for diseases caused by bacteria and other germs. For example, doctors once thought that tuberculosis had been all but wiped out in the United States. They were wrong. Tuberculosis is back. The scary part is that antibiotics and other drugs long used to treat people with tuberculosis no longer appear to be effective in all cases. A new strain of the disease has become resistant to the drugs. Malaria is another disease that has made a deadly comeback. Once again, this mosquito-carried disease is killing millions worldwide with renewed vigor.

The most depressing part of the story is that HIV has mutated into forms that are resistant to every kind of antiretroviral drug tested in people so far. This grim fact caused researchers to try a new strategy. To defeat HIV using drugs, scientists decided to bombard the virus with many different kinds of drugs all at once. The hope is that HIV will not be able to mutate fast enough to become resistant to each individual part of this chemical cocktail at one time. The problem now facing scientists is finding a fast way to figure out which drugs work together the best. Some drugs cause harmful side effects in some people. A drug that kills or makes a patient extremely sick is not much better than the disease it is designed to fight.

Scientists searching for new anti-AIDS drugs now are trying a "shotgun" approach. The idea is to combine a handful of promising drugs that have shown fewer harmful side effects. They want to see if such a combination helps HIV-infected people. But other scientists argue that this approach might speed HIV's resistance to one or all of these drugs.

In another large area of research, scientists selectively study chemicals and compounds that work against various parts of HIV's life cycle. The idea is to develop a drug that interrupts HIV's ability to reproduce itself at different stages. If scientists could throw chemical wrenches into the machinery that HIV uses to reproduce itself, the virus simply would not be able to make enough copies of itself to keep the disease going inside an infected person's body. Such drugs could also increase the time it takes for the virus to become resistant to any single drug, allowing researchers more time to find a permanent cure.

Hope from Protease Inhibitors

HIV makes new copies of itself by hijacking the genetic machinery of immune system T4 cells or other host cells. During one of the final steps in the complex process, long chains of proteins and enzymes must be cut into smaller pieces. Protease is the chemical "scissors" HIV uses to cut these chains into shorter pieces. Protease inhibitors are drugs meant to be lookalikes. The drugs resemble pieces of the protein chain that HIV protease normally cuts. By clogging up the protease scissors, HIV protease inhibitors prevent protease from cutting the long protein chains and enzymes into shorter pieces. Without the smaller pieces, HIV cannot make new infectious copies of itself.

The new drugs do not completely stop HIV from reproducing. Even if all of the long protein chains are not cut into the correct size smaller bits, the infected cell still manages to produce new copies of HIV. Without the short pieces of protein, however, these copies are defective. They cannot infect other cells. The strategy is simple enough. If the drugs succeed in making large numbers of new HIV particles defective, scientists believe that HIV infection will not spread as quickly in the body. Patients will live longer, perhaps long enough for a cure to be found.

While results from early studies indicate that protease inhibitors can reduce the amount of virus by as much as 99 percent, scientists know that some HIV remains tucked safely inside other cells that are not actively producing new virus. These "dormant" or "latently infected" cells may live undetected for years. Scientists doubt that any one drug or combination of drugs could kill or disable all the virus in an infected person. Still, with less virus, fewer T4 cells are infected, fewer cells die, and the HIV patient can stay healthier longer.

Several protease inhibitors are now being used in the United States. Most are being used in combination with reverse transcriptase inhibiting drugs like AZT and 3TC. The new drugs are called indinavir, ritonavir, and saquinavir. It is too early to tell which combinations work best. Different combinations may work better for different people. Like many strong chemical medications, protease inhibitors also cause nasty side effects such as nausea and diarrhea.

The Search for a Vaccine

The solution that most scientists dream of is the development of a vaccine for AIDS. An effective vaccine will be key to slowing the epidemic, especially in resource-poor countries in the developing world that cannot afford expensive drug treatments.

"A safe and effective vaccine against HIV is critical to our efforts to control the global AIDS pandemic," says Dr. Anthony Fauci, director of the U.S. National Institute for Allergy and Infectious Disease. The NIAID provides funding to support research by scientists throughout the world.

Fooling the immune system is not an easy task, but that is exactly what a successful vaccine must do. A vaccine is nothing more than an artificially created impostor. Vaccines are harmless mimics that are meant to be identified by the body as vicious enemies. When the scam works, the vaccine forces the immune system through a crash course in self-defense. We know that the immune system has the ability to remember microbes it has fought and defeated. If a vaccine works and the immune system learns its lesson well, the body is ready when real disease-causing invaders appear.

Once again, however, HIV does not follow the normal rules. HIV is an incredibly elusive virus. It mutates rapidly into subtle new forms. Researchers have a tough time keeping up with HIV's ability to change its protein face.

What scientists do know is that unlike most viruses, HIV can be transmitted as either a free virus or inside infected cells. This means that infection can spread by cell-to-cell contact. When in working order, the immune system fights free viruses by producing antibodies that are custom-made to attach to the virus. Once attached, they render the virus harmless or mark it for destruction by killer cells. But antibodies do not work against

HIV-infected cells because they can't tell the cells are infected. Direct action of immune system cells against these virus-infected cells is needed. Scientists think that both types of immune response are necessary to protect the body against HIV infection.

Will Vaccines Work against HIV?

Vaccines are not magical solutions. Perhaps we are spoiled. During the twentieth century, medical science developed effective vaccines against old scourges that once killed millions of people. Of course, there are no vaccines against the common cold, which is caused by a type of virus known as rhinovirus. Like HIV, rhinoviruses mutate much too quickly for any one vaccine ever to be effective against them. Despite all that we

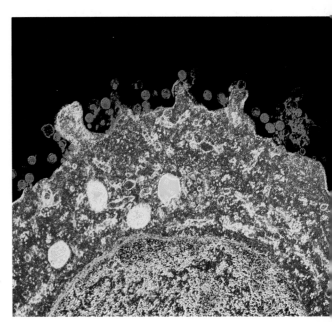

One mutation of HIV—HIV-2— has changed so much that scientists gave it another name.

know, there are huge scientific problems that must be over-come before any effective vaccine for rhinoviruses or HIV can be developed. Realistically, many scientists think that a vaccine for HIV may never work.

The first big problem in designing a vaccine is safety. Vaccines are designed to prevent disease in healthy people. Researchers know that infection with a mild strain of a virus often shields against a future bout with a related strain. That is the strategy behind flu vaccines. In most cases, vaccines are weakened versions of the disease-causing microbe itself. Sometimes vaccines are made of dead virus. The weakened or dead germs are given to a person to sensitize the immune system.

For a disease such as the flu, people are given a solution that contains a killed or weakened form of the virus. Occasionally, people get sick from the vaccine. However, with flu vaccines, the result is not normally deadly. AIDS is very different. The safety factor is not yet controllable. Injecting a person with intact HIV is an unacceptable risk. As a result, scientists are trying to get around the problem by making a vaccine from bits and pieces of the protein coat that surrounds HIV. Isolated from the whole, these bits and pieces are themselves not capable of causing infection. The hope is that these parts will be enough to teach the immune system to switch into action when it meets the entire AIDS virus.

Another major safety barrier has to do with testing. Scientists have to follow precise procedures in order to be sure that a vaccine really works. In the case of AIDS, to be sure a vaccine really is effective, at least some of the test subjects would have to continue to engage in high-risk behavior that exposes them to infection after they have been vaccinated. Is such action moral? Is such testing scientifically ethical? What are the legal ramifications if the vaccine fails? Could the scientists be held responsible for giving a healthy person a deadly disease?

If indeed a vaccine for AIDS were developed, a look at the history of medical science tells us that it probably would not be 100 percent effective. In many populations of people where the disease is already widespread, scientists know that many people constantly are reexposed to the virus. Using a vaccine to stop AIDS in such populations might be the same as having no vaccine at all.

Finally, vaccines are very expensive to make. They are even more difficult to distribute to huge numbers of people. Measles, mumps, whooping cough, and other childhood diseases could have been wiped out in the United States many years ago. The vaccines against these diseases are very effective, but many people do not get their children vaccinated. As a result, these diseases are making a strong comeback in this country.

Despite the obstacles, scientists continue to work to develop vaccines against HIV. Dozens of different vaccines are currently at different stages of development. The first major tests of two human vaccines began in 1998.

Rebuilding the Immune System

Some researchers think that all the work on vaccines and new drugs to battle HIV is a waste of time and money. They propose using a dramatic new approach called gene therapy. Gene therapy harnesses the emerging power of genetic engineering techniques. Described in basic terms, the idea is to rebuild immune systems that have been wrecked by the virus. The idea is intriguing and has many supporters, but scientists simply do not know enough about the powerful techniques of gene manipulation to put them to work against HIV. Yet.

Researchers in many countries are moving forward to develop these powerful new techniques into a method of treatment and cure. In one strategy, scientists propose inserting protective new genes into the immune system cells that HIV normally infects. In theory, these new genes would combat HIV by producing proteins that disrupt the inner workings of the virus itself. The idea is to turn the tables on HIV by infecting it with material that wrecks its ability to reproduce.

Another gene therapy technique being considered by scientists is called the "kamikaze approach." Kamikazes were Japanese pilots who flew suicide missions during World War II. The kamikazes flew planes loaded with explosives and crashed them directly into American warships. Using the kamikaze approach against HIV, scientists plan to insert a "poison gene" directly into healthy T4 cells and other HIV targets. This gene would turn on only if the cells become infected by HIV. Once infected, the cells would self-destruct before their genetic machinery could be taken over by HIV. In essence, the idea is to program cells to commit suicide if they become infected, before they can spread the disease.

Another idea is to outfit white blood cells called suppressor cells with new genes. These suppressor cells would make the proteins that are ordinarily produced by the T4 cells. As a result, the suppressor cells would partially take over the duties of their HIV-stricken cousins. The hope is that the immune system would continue to function, on some levels, with the help of the T4 cell replacements.

Into an Unknown World

Genetic engineering and gene therapy have long been the stuff of science fiction. No longer. The techniques are scientific reality. But genetic engineering is controversial. Critics say that humans should not tinker with nature. Supporters, however, hail genetic engineering and gene therapy as the most exciting medical developments since the discovery of penicillin and other antibiotics. The critics argue that the manipulation of genetic material is not a power to be trifled with. Many scientists say that such power must be governed by a great sense of responsibility and strict rules of use. Using gene therapy, physicians and scientists are manipulating the genetic blueprints of all life on Earth. For some, such power calls to mind images of Dr. Frankenstein and his monster; hideous half-man, half-beasts found in *The Island of Dr. Moreau*; or the clones of Aldous Huxley's *Brave New World* made a reality.

Gene therapy is the result of two recent leaps in modern genetics. Scientists now have the ability to identify specific fragments of DNA that are the recipes for making proteins. They also can identify DNA fragments that control whether or not other genes will produce the proteins that they are coded to produce. More important, researchers now have effective techniques for inserting those DNA fragments into disarmed viruses. They use these viruses as biological shuttles to transport specific bits of DNA directly into living cells. All this is done right in the laboratory. Scientists no longer have to wait an entire generation to right a genetic wrong. Whether this new power can be used to defeat HIV remains to be seen.

No End in Sight

One of the major barricades to stopping the spread of AIDS is the unwillingness of some governments to admit that the disease is a problem in their countries. Politics and medicine never have been a productive mix. Medical scientists are into their second decade studying and dealing with HIV and AIDS. In the early 1980s, there was an era of naive optimism about what science and technology could achieve quickly. As the decade progressed, that thinking swung to a bleak pessimism—we were all doomed. Reality is probably somewhere in between.

The new protease inhibitor drugs introduced in 1996 could become the first real success story in treating the disease. Unfortunately, these new drugs are complicated to use. Patients must take as many as 30 different pills each day in a specific order and at specific intervals. The drugs produce some serious side effects. They are so expensive that very few patients can afford to pay for the treatment. Treating 2,500 patients at one hospital with a three-drug combination and monitoring their HIV levels is estimated to cost $22 million per year. This expense rules out most patients in the United States. It definitely puts such treatment out of reach to the more than 20 million HIV-infected people living in Africa and Asia. Scientists are quick to note that while protease inhibitor drugs appear to work well in the short term, we must wait to see whether or not they remain effective against the disease over time.

Researchers are focusing new studies on the tiny fraction of people infected with HIV who remain healthy for years. The scientists want to learn how the bodies of these few people fight off the onset of AIDS. Finding that information may be key to developing methods for helping the millions of others infected with the virus. More importantly, that knowledge may provide the key to preventing infection in healthy people.

Of course, breakthroughs could occur at any time. But most medical researchers are conservative. The road ahead in the search for an AIDS cure or the development of effective HIV vaccines is probably still a long one.

In September 1996, the head of the United Nations AIDS program delivered a sobering message tinged with a bit of optimism to those attending the eleventh International Conference on AIDS in Vancouver. Dr. Peter Piot told more than 15,000 researchers, patients, journalists, and AIDS activists that the world must face the fact that AIDS is no longer simply an outbreak. "AIDS has become entrenched and will be an integral part of the human condition for a very long time to come," Piot said. He called the epidemic "huge, unstable, and mainly invisible."

Scientists appreciate just how powerful a foe the AIDS virus really is. In addition to seeking a vaccine or a cure for infection with HIV, greater effort is needed to teach people how to prevent themselves from catching the virus.

In late 1997, the World Health Organization estimated that almost 31 million people were already infected with HIV. If the virus continues to spread at the same rate, between 40 and 110 million people would be infected before the year 2000. But that number could increase considerably if the disease were to take hold in Asia, where it seems to be spreading the fastest. The majority of HIV infections—more than 27 million—have occurred in developing countries. Until recently, HIV was rare in countries such as China and Indonesia. The disease already is entrenched in India, Thailand, Burma, and other countries with huge populations. More than half of the almost 6 billion people living on earth live in Asia. WHO says that the number of HIV-infected people in Southern and Southeast Asia is now more than twice the total number of those infected in the entire industrialized world. Worldwide, WHO estimates that 11.7 million people have already died from AIDS.

With no cure in sight, health officials believe a few basic

strategies can help to stop the spread of the disease—more and better education on safe sexual practices, promoting the use of condoms, and better treatment of existing sexually transmitted diseases (STDs). Infection with other STDs makes HIV easier to catch and transmit to others. Scientists have learned that infections with other organisms, especially those responsible for other STDs, activate the immune system cells and increase the production of the virus in HIV-infected people. A more active virus makes infection more likely.

In August 1994, Dr. Hiroshi Nakajima, the director-general of WHO, told those attending the AIDS conference that "fear, indifference and denial, along with poverty, are the main enemies" in the effort to control AIDS in the world.

Public health officials and schools need to reemphasize prevention techniques. They must continue to debunk the many recurring myths about this killer disease. HIV is transmitted through bodily fluids, especially blood, semen, and vaginal secretions. There is absolutely no evidence that the disease can be transmitted by casual contact. Unprotected sex is especially dangerous. But there is no such thing as a risk-free condom.

It is precisely before the virus gets inside the body that people have the most control of preventing the spread of AIDS. It is up to you to stop HIV before it ever has the chance to get inside your body. Stopping HIV is easy, if you are smart and follow a few simple precautions. If you are careless, or like taking risks, you are risking more than just catching a disease. You are risking your life and the lives of others.

There is one good, effective strategy that each one of us can put to work every day to slow the spread of AIDS. Each one of us can arm the ones we love with the most up-to-date information we can find. Children, teenagers, and adults must learn

Knowing how HIV works, it's possible to keep it from infecting the ones we love.

the correct information about HIV and AIDS. The disease can infect anyone, heterosexuals and homosexuals alike. It can infect people of every race and ethnic background.

AIDS is not a secret. AIDS is a killer disease that is loose and spreading among the 6 billion human beings living on this planet. AIDS is a preventable disease. The spread of HIV infection can be stopped. Stopping it is up to each and every one of us. Teenagers can play a huge role in stopping this killer, by making it a priority to learn all there is to know about HIV and AIDS prevention, especially at the beginning of your sexual lives. Once sexual activity does begin, make sure you fully understand the risks you are taking if you do not practice safe sex. We have to learn to be smarter than the disease. We have only ourselves to blame if we let HIV infect us or the ones we love.

Glossary

antibodies—specialized protein molecules produced and secreted by certain types of white cells in response to stimulation by an antigen. They attack and destroy specific microbes that invade the body.

antigen—any substance that triggers an immune response because the body recognizes it as foreign. Antigens can be a virus, a bacterium, or even a portion or product of such organisms.

autoantibody—an antibody that reacts against a person's own healthy tissue

bone marrow—soft tissue found in the hollow center of bones. Bone marrow is the site where all blood cells, red and white, are produced.

bacteria—single-celled living organisms

B cells—white blood cells of the immune system produced in bone marrow and involved in the production of antibodies

chromosome—microscopic, threadlike structures that are found in the nucleus of each plant or animal cell. They contain DNA, the basic material of heredity.

DNA (deoxyribonucleic acid)—the long, twisted molecule in a cell's chromosomes that contains the genetic information that is passed from parents to their young

enzymes—proteins that help or drive chemical reactions in the body

gene—a segment of DNA that is the basic unit of heredity. Each gene provides coded instructions for one or more hereditary traits.

hemophilia—an inherited condition in which blood does not clot normally. People with hemophilia need transfusions of blood products to stay healthy.

helper T cells—T4 cells. They help control immune system function by sending other cells or chemicals to fight an invader.

HIV (human immunodeficiency virus)—the virus that causes AIDS

immune system—a system of organs, cells-especially white blood cells-and chemicals that work together to fight disease lymph—a clear fluid that bathes the body's tissues

lymph nodes—small, bean-shaped structures that are clustered in the neck, armpits, abdomen, and groin. Each node is found at a junction of many lymph vessels. They contain special sections where immune system cells collect and encounter antigens.

lymphocytes—small white cells, normally present in the blood. They bear the major responsibility for carrying out the functions of the immune system.

lymph system—a network of small vessels, much like blood vessels, that carry lymph throughout the body. Immune system cells, such as lymphocytes and macrophages, move through the lymph system as well as through the blood.

macrophage—from the Greek word meaning "big eater," white blood cells that form part of the first line of defense, attacking all foreign invaders and carrying parts of the invader back to the T cells. Macrophages also help clean up after the invaders are destroyed.

microbes—living organisms that are invisible except under a microscope

protease inhibitors—medicines that stop the work of the enzyme protease

proteins—molecules that are necessary in all living matter and are the essential compounds of the immune system

retrovirus—a virus with an RNA core rather than a DNA core

RNA (ribonucleic acid)—the long, twisted molecule that helps copy a cell's DNA

suppresser cells—T cells that help control immune system function by holding back immune units from fighting an invader, keeping a balance with the helper T cells

T cells—white blood cells processed in the thymus. They produce lymphokines and are responsible, in large part, for carrying out the immune response.

virus—the smallest and simplest of all life forms

For Further Information

Up-to-date information about HIV and AIDS can be found on the World Wide Web. Here are a few sites and addresses to get you started:

AIDS Clinical Trial Information Service
http://www.actis.org

This website and organization "provides current information on federally and privately sponsored clinical trials for persons with AIDS and HIV infection."

> PO Box 6421
> Rockville, MD 20849-6421
> 1-800-trials-a
> email: actis@cdnac.org

AIDS Handbook for Middle School Kids
http://www.westnet.com/~rickd/AIDS1.htm

"Written by middle school kids, for middle school kids," this site also deals with the topic of AIDS for younger people. It links to pages on AIDS prevention and transmission (among other topics).

AIDS Information for Teenagers
http://www.avert.org/young.htm

This is a good resource for basic information about AIDS. It also has a search option to look into a topic in more depth, as well as links to specific AIDS-related topics.

Centers for Disease Control and Prevention
http://www.cdc.gov

This website has a search option for specific topics that may be in the website. It also hosts a health information directory that, if clicked on, will lead to an HIV/AIDS page at *http://www.cdc.gov/diseases/hivqa.html,* which in turn links to several AIDS-related topics.

> 1600 Clifton Road, NE
> Atlanta, GA 30333
> (404)639-3311

HIV/AIDS Treatment Information Service

http://www.hivatis.org

This website "provides information about federally approved treatment guidelines for HIV and AIDS."

    PO Box 6303
    Rockville, MD 20849-6303
    1-800-HIV-0440
    email: atis@cdnac.org

Journal of the American Medical Association (JAMA)
HIV/AIDS Information Center

http://www.ama.assn.org/special/hiv/hivhome.htm

This website links to information about prevention and treatment. Especially helpful is a link to Best of the Net, a list of websites on AIDS that JAMA most recommends. The JAMA AIDS/HIV Best of the Net pages are at *http://www.ama.assn.org/special/hiv/bestonet/bestonet.htm*

National Institutes of Health

http://www.nih.gov

This website also has its own search engine to look up specific information. In addition, it links to an OAR (Office of AIDS Research) website at *http://www/nih.gov/od/oar/index.htm*. The OAR website includes a directory of topics related to the organization and what it is doing.

    Bethesda, MD 20892
    (301)496-1766
    OAR is located in the Office of the Director at NIH

World Health Organization (WHO)

http://www.who.org

The WHO website includes a search tool to look for specific information within the site. The regional WHO office for the Americas has its own website and regular address. It is the Pan American Health Organization (PAHO) at *http://www.paho.org*, which links to the PAHO Program on AIDS/STD at *http://www.paho.org/english./aid/aidstd.htm*.

    Pan American Health Organization
    Regional Office of the World Health Organization
    525 Twenty Third St. NW
    Washington, DC 20037
    (202)974-3000

Index

Joint United Nations Program on HIV/AIDS, 8

Kamikaze approach, 84
Kaposi's sarcoma, 70
Koch, Robert, 41–43

lymph nodes, 52, 54
lymph system, 25, 29, 51, 54–55
lymphocytes, 25, 27

macrophages, 29, 30, 51–52, 54–55
malaria, 43, 77
media, 14
medicine. *See* drugs, AIDS
membrane, 21–22, 23, 45–46
microbes, 24, 28, 30, 31, 41–42, 51
mitochondria, 23
molecules, 23, 24, 27, 30, 45–46
monkeys, 16
monocytes, 29
Montagnier, Luc, 15
mucus, 51, 61

Nakajima, Hiroshi, 88
nonself cells, 30–31
nucleic acid core, 34
nucleotides, 37
nucleus, 22, 23, 37

opportunistic infections, 31, 69
organelles, 22, 23–24

parvovirus, 45
Pasteur Institute, 15
Pasteur, Louis, 41
pathogens, 41
phagocytes, 29
pigs, 39–40
Piot, Peter, 87
Pneumocystis carinii pneumonia (PCP), 13, 70
polio, 43
politics, 85
prevention, 9, 61–73
protease inhibitors, 75, 78–79, 86

protein, 22, 23, 27, 30, 34, 37–38, 45–46, 57, 67, 79
research, 7–9, 16–17, 53, 58–59, 74–89
retroviruses, 37–38, 45
reverse transcriptase, 38, 76, 79
ribosomes, 23
RNA (ribonucleic acid), 37–38, 46, 50

self cells, 30–31, 54
semen, 62, 88
sex, 8, 14, 62, 65, 88
smallpox, 39, 43, 45
source of infection, 8, 64–66, 89
Spanish flu, 39–40
spread of AIDS, 17, 19, 62–66, 87–89
statistics, 8, 11–12, 17–19
suppressor cells, 84
symptoms, 69–73

T cells, 25–28, 30, 31, 50–51, 52, 57, 59
T4 cells, 27, 45, 52, 55, 59, 62, 76
T8 cells, 27
testing for HIV, 66–69
thrush, 71–72
tobacco mosaic disease, 42
transcriptase, 37
tuberculosis, 43, 77

U.S. Armed Forces Institute of Pathology, 39
U.S. National Cancer Institute (NCI), 15, 75–76

vaccines, 81–83
vaginal secretions, 62, 88
viruses, 33–43, 45, 51, 61

Western blot, 67, 68
World Health Organization (WHO), 11, 19, 73, 87

About the Author

Conrad J. Storad is director of the Office of Research Publications at Arizona State University, where he edits and writes for the nationally award winning *ASU Research Magazine* and coordinates the production of the magazine's TV version, "ASU Research Review." He is also the author of several science books for children and young adults, including the Lerner Publications titles *Saguaro Cactus, Scorpions,* and *Tarantulas.* Storad is a member of the National Association of Science Writers, the Society of Children's Book Writers and Illustrators, and the International Association of Business Communicators, and has served two terms as president of the University Research Magazine Association. He lives in Tempe, Arizona, but often goes in search of big rainbow trout in Wyoming and Montana.

Photo Acknowledgments

The photographs have been reproduced with the permission of: © David M. Phillips/Visuals Unlimited, pp. 2-3, 10, 21, 33, 45, 61, 74; © NIBSC/Science Photo Library/Photo Researchers, Inc. (P.R.I.), pp. 3 (inset), 56; © Leonard Lessin/Peter Arnold, Inc., p. 6; © Hans Gelderblom/Visuals Unlimited, pp. 12, 32; N.C.I./Science Source/P.R.I., p. 15; © Mehau Kulyk/Science Photo Library/ P.R.I., p. 20; © Kenneth Eward/Science Source/P.R.I., p. 22; © Secchi, Lecaque, Roussel, UCLAF, CNRI/Science Photo Library/P.R.I., p. 25; © Dr. J. Ortaldo/ Peter Arnold, Inc., pp. 26 (both), 27; © Biology Media/Science Source/P.R.I., p. 29; © Alfred Pasieka/Peter Arnold, Inc., p. 40; © K. G. Murti/Visuals Unlimited, p. 43; © Manfred Kage/Peter Arnold, Inc., p. 44; NIAID, National Institutes of Health, p. 50; © Dr. Arnold Brody/Science Photo Library/P.R.I., p. 52; © Barry Dowsett/Science Photo Library/P.R.I., p. 53; © Comstock, Inc, cover inset, p. 60; © Ed Kashi, p. 63 (bottom); © CC Studio/Science Photo Library/P.R.I., pp. 63 (top); © Hank Morgan/Science Source/P.R.I., pp. 66, 67; © Sue Ford/Science Photo Library/P.R.I., p. 71 (left); © Zeva Delbaum/Peter Arnold, Inc., p. 71 (right); © Dr. P. Marrazzi/Science Photo Library/P.R.I., p. 72; National Cancer Institute, p. 77; © University of Medicine and Dentistry of New Jersey/Science Photo Library/P.R.I., p. 81; © Brian Yarvin/Peter Arnold, Inc., p. 89.

Illustrations on pp. 35-36, 38, 46, 47-49, courtesy of Laura Westlund.

Cover photograph reproduced with the permission of NIBSC/Science Photo Library and cover inset reproduced with the permission of © Comstock, Inc.